A GLOVE ON MY HEART

ENCOUNTERS WITH
THE MENTALLY ILL

A Glove on My Heart

Judith Reynolds Brown

2001 PeaceWorks International

I would like to offer thanks to several people for their support during the writing of *A Glove on My Heart*.

First, I thank the clients I worked with who so readily spoke with me and gave me their trust. Their friendship and antics moved me to write poetry about them. It was those poems with which the book began, but when I asked Nancy Rekow to look at the poems and offer suggestions, it was she who persuaded me to write the prose that accompanies them. The prose, I hope, puts the poetry in context for a wider audience. Jerry Schoenberg read the manuscript and offered support with his initial editing, and Eric Larson's know-how and final editing was invaluable. David Johnson encouraged me at every stage of the writing, as did Perry Wien.

Finally, I am very much indebted to the knowledge and encouragement of my husband, Jack Ross Brown, M.D., without whose patience and support the book never would have been written.

Printed in the United States of America

Published by PeaceWorks International
Post Office Box 591
East Olympia, WA 98540

Book design & production: Studio E Books, Santa Barbara, California

LIBRARY OF CONGRESS CATALOGING IN PUBLICATION DATA
Brown, Judith Reynolds, (date)
A glove on my heart : encounters with the mentally ill / by Judith Reynolds Brown.
p. cm.
ISBN 0-9705664-0-9 (pbk.)
1. Group homes for the mentally ill—Washington (State)—Case studies.
2. Mentally ill. 3. Mentally ill—Poetry. 4. Mental illness. 5. Mentall illness—Poetry. 6. Volunteer workers in mental health. 7. Brown, Judith Reynolds, (date)
I. Title.
RC439.55 .B76 2001
305.9'0824--dc21

00-012213

CONTENTS

FOREWORD

Present-Day Treatment of Chronic Mental Illness

by DAVID M. JOHNSON, ED.D.

IN EACH AND EVERY community of humans since the beginning of recorded history we find indications that every tribe has had to find a way to deal with the manifestations which we understand, in our culture, to be mental illnesses. For those who have been terrorized by psychotic delusions and hallucinations or immobilized by deadening depression, each culture has sought an explanation and then based treatment on that conceptualization.

In societies who perceived these symptoms to be indications of moral and spiritual weaknesses, there have been spiritual remedies ranging from sustained prayer to cutting holes in the skull through which evil spirits could escape. Societies who have explained the symptoms as gifts of visions from the gods have exalted and revered those affected and have sought the poetic meaning in their oblique proclamations. When mental illnesses have been understood to be results of fatigue, cures have been sought in sustained respite, sleep, baths, and meditation. Those who have believed that psychosis, depression, or mania were the results of childhood trauma or confounding family dynamics have sought cures through analysis of childhood memories. Though traumatic experience can nudge an individual toward more psychological distress, such experiences don't create physically based disorders like schizophrenia or bipolar illness.

At various points throughout history there has been intrigue in the possibility that the symptoms of what we call today the major mental illnesses (gross thought disorders such as schizophrenia and mood disorders such as clinical depression and bipolar illness) have physical causes. Indeed, one percent of any population found around the globe exhibits clinically diagnosable schizophrenia, a fact so consistent that it defies culturally specific "bad parenting" theories and parallels other epidemiological syndromes. Recent research has shown that the brain structures, synaptic functioning, and blood chemistries of individuals with major illnesses are consistently different from those of individuals without such symptoms, and like those of other people with similar symptoms. Though considered a radical idea just a few decades ago, there is clear agreement among most responsible and effective clinicians today that major mental illnesses have physiological bases, just like diabetes and heart disease, and that the core of treatment needs to incorporate physiological interventions.

Though today we may share with some ancient and medieval cultures the same belief that major mental illnesses have physiological bases, our physiological treatments differ from those of the past. We no longer use leeches for bloodletting nor the blunt surgeries of centuries ago. Research is evermore rapidly defining which sites in the brain have various structures and which receptor sites in the synapses of the complex neurological web of the brain need intervention to ensure an adequate amount of specific transmitters to allow the individual to function effectively.

We still have far to go in being able to medicate people so that the symptoms are addressed in ways that do not have severe side effects that cause yet other problems and other symptoms in trade, yet we are amazingly further along than we might have expected as recently as a decade ago.

Our previous generation of antipsychotic medications did, in the grossest measures, block out the most frightening psychotic impulses of many patients, though many others never showed any response to those medications. Yet the price paid was a sluggish and dispirited existence and the threat of long-term or permanent neurological damage (tardive dyskinesia) that appeared worse than the initial disease itself. New antipsychotic medications are now far more successful in treating the primary symptoms of thought disorders (e.g. delusions and hallucinations) as well as the secondary symptoms (e.g. inappropriate social interactions and decline in personal hygiene) and do so without risk of tardive dyskinesia.

However, they bear their own risks of disturbing side effects: huge weight gain in some, or risk of damage to the white blood cells.

Our previous generation of mood-stabilizing medications helped many to avoid the suicidal lows and the dangerous manic highs that have devastated so many lives, yet again with a price to be paid in gross side effects. The new medications are more specific in their physiological interventions, maximizing effects without needlessly affecting other physiological functioning. However, even these new medications have debilitating side effects for some. Still other individuals have symptoms that remain unabated, despite all the possible medication regimes we can devise to try to help them. Even though we have such certainty that physiological interventions are crucial to treating major mental illnesses, there are many practical day-to-day needs of those with these illnesses that biochemical remedies don't address. Where does one live who must be so delicately careful of her biochemical state? How does she support herself, and her very expensive medical costs, when full-time work is not possible even with the best medications? How can families who love these people so intensely still go about their daily business and tend to those who are not so afflicted? How do we ward off the devastation that substance abuse has on people who already have such remarkable biochemical imbalances?

In the 1960s and 1970s, as the first family of medications seemed so promising, politicians, clinicians, and lay citizens alike championed the huge process of deinstitutionalization, thinking that daily medications and outpatient hospital programs would keep patients stabilized. We moved people with major mental illnesses out of the warehouses of state institutions and back into "the community," which all too often actually meant large, substandard boarding homes in frightening sections of metropolitan areas.

The secret assumption and motivation was that taxpayers would get a break from the expensive twenty-four-hour hospital supervision. The tragic result has been observed by all who live in cities: people with major mental illnesses of course stopped taking the medications that offered such uncomfortable side effects. Many quickly decompensated and repeatedly recycled through the local emergency rooms and state institutions. Many others became homeless and floated for years in a miasma of mental illness and substance abuse and the vulnerability to victimization and crime that are such a part of life on the streets.

Many family members, some public servants, and some charitable organizations moved ambitiously into the breech left by the poorly planned debacle of deinstitutionalization. They developed alternatives to the simple formula of warehouse plus gross medication. The founding of TRY House in the 1970s is an example. Developed by a particularly visionary set of volunteers, TRY House was designed to be a small, intentional community in which those with mental illnesses would be as autonomous as possible in governing and operating their own home, doing what adults do in terms of shopping, cooking, cleaning, and finding meaning in productive work and relationships. Through the years, as new medications made it possible for even more severely ill individuals to be maintained in the community, TRY House has served an increasingly less functional clientele. The core values of the organization have not changed, though, and even to this day the milieu and norms of the community of TRY House shape the members into being as self-reliant as possible, contributing as best they can to the good of the household.

This focus on the capacity and dignity of even the most disabled individual is far more expensive, time-consuming, and challenging than the simple warehousing of disabled people. It is obvious that the average American taxpayer and typical legislator are not willing to allot the necessary funds to treat all those in need with the level of services that is most effective and most respectful. It is doubtful that this society will ever be so giving to this population whom those who do not understand, those who do not have mentally ill family members, find so frightening and distasteful.

Staff in mental health treatment programs work first to stabilize the mentally ill individual, usually monitoring a medication regime, finding ongoing funding for the individual, working to coordinate other medical and social services, allying with the families to establish round-the-clock networks of support. Next, staff seek to find meaningful work, whether paid or volunteer, through which the mentally ill adult can be a contributing member of the community. Tediously, the staff must also document every iota of care they give to meet the amazing bureaucracy of oversight that is attached to the expenditure of all public funds. At times it seems that for every hour of service given, there is a half-hour of paperwork needed to justify that service.

In order for places like TRY House to succeed, they must rely heavily on charitable funding and volunteers to subsidize the inadequate public resources that are meagerly apportioned to them. One fortunately wonderful element of relying on volunteers is that the quality of person who tends to be such a volunteer is outstanding. The compassion, dedication to social justice, and respect for the dignity of the afflicted such a volunteer tends to exhibit are greatly moving and powerful.

This book tells the story of what is possible when compassion and respect guide the provision of pragmatic care. It shows how we can honor those with mental illness when our effort is to witness first and foremost the goodness, the humanness, and the valor of their aspirations to live their lives meaningfully despite their great disabilities.

David M. Johnson, Ed.D. is President and CEO of West Seattle Psychiatric Hospital and Highline/West Seattle Mental Health Center.

PREFACE

A RECEPTIONIST in my husband's office used to ask those who inquired about psychiatric services, "Are you new to mental health?"

I thought her question was apt and was only put off when her phrase became the butt of office jokes. If she'd asked me I would have said, "Yes, and I'm afraid of the mentally ill." That wouldn't have been the answer she wanted, but it would have been honest.

When I had reached my late sixties, not much about the human world seemed new anymore, and I wanted it to. I craved a different kind of adventure, a place where I could use my skills as a person, not my professional experience as an English teacher. I've counted on new experiences in my life to expand my world. The idea of an adventure with persons who were mentally ill, learning a knack—the knack of how one relates to them in a natural, caring way—seemed an intriguing challenge.

I am not a physician, nor am I a therapist. But I'm married to a physician therapist who spent many years in a psychiatric practice. I knew he had used a great deal of psychopharmacology in his practice and felt the general public did not yet understand how useful psychotropic drugs could be to the mentally ill. Where could I go to volunteer where persons were housed, medicated, and treated well?

Before he retired, my husband claimed to enjoy working with persons who were severely handicapped mentally almost more than he enjoyed doing therapy with those who were merely troubled and hoped to emerge from their therapy vastly improved. I had always been curious about what he meant. Armed with that curiosity and knowing of a small treatment center licensed to provide good care for the mentally ill in Seattle, I decided to take the plunge. What kind of program did a "good" home offer? I wanted to be able to advocate effectively for more good homes for the mentally ill. In the end, however, to observe a well-run home for the mentally ill turned out not to be the point. In the end my years' *experience* volunteering full time turned out to be infinitely more rewarding than any *knowledge* I gained.

A "cure," my husband had said many times, "is not what the therapist is after when dealing with mental illness." The severely mentally ill hope for something less ambitious: to be more comfortable with themselves, to have better coping skills, to have less anguish, to be able to get through their days with a modicum of competence. All psychiatric patients are somehow seeking a kind of "healing" in the broad sense.

However, I observed that the ways one works to help severely handicapped clients vary. My husband had claimed that one needs to establish a relationship with the severely mentally ill. A severely ill person has to be persuaded by that relationship to want to cope. That same relationship can build confidence—make a mentally ill person feel he or she *can* cope. The mentally ill also need to see the value of taking their medications. Such a therapeutic relationship requires letting a client know you care, and caring can't be faked. Practicing caring is part of what I've been about as an adult—with my children, my parents, and certain friends. Therapy, I knew I wasn't trained to do. But caring seemed possible.

Having read Oliver Sacks's *Awakenings*, I was also influenced by his approach to writing about his patients. In his earliest preface, Sacks says about his book:

> Running throughout the book is a metaphysical theme—the notion that it is insufficient to consider disease in purely mechanical or chemical terms; that it must be considered equally in biological or metaphysical terms, i.e. in terms of organization and design.... In present day medicine...there is an almost exclusively technical or mechanical emphasis, which has led to immense advances, but also to intellectual regression, and a lack of proper attention to the full needs and feelings of patients.

I knew of a private non-profit mental health agency that housed fifteen persons. This agency required its residents to be psychiatrically treated and medicated, but at the same time it tried to pay "proper attention to the full needs and feelings" of the people under its care—people who had come to a point in their mental illnesses where they needed to live somewhere with more support than they were able to get at home, if they had homes. The executive director of this agency was a personal friend. Having helped to found this agency in the late 70s, my husband was still on its board of directors. I knew the house made use of full-time volunteers on a limited stipend. Twelve years after I retired from teaching gifted students, and after a good deal of work abroad, I was ready for something new in these United States. The executive director turned out to be open to my experimental mood, and I began, committing myself for a full year.

When I had worked for a while at the agency, my husband reminded me of another aspect of mental illness that Sacks had suggested in *Awakenings*. Often, in his experience, when medication has helped a mentally ill person control his or her particular disease, the client is still left with his or her own idiosyncratic characteristics, be they lethargy, gentility, irascibility, sweetness, generosity or whatever. I should count on those idiosyncrasies, he suggested, to influence the ease or difficulty of establishing a relationship with the residents with whom I worked.

In the course of my year's work I found myself wanting to keep a journal in which I recorded experiences with the residents. I knew that presenting these persons in image and vignette would make them more appealing. I wanted to present them as intriguing, colorful people rather than people it would be awkward to know. I commuted to the house from our island by ferry, and the half-hour ride to and from the city was a good time to make brief notations. What came out on those ferry rides were poems rather than stories. This account then, a true account of real people (in which I've not used real names), will be peppered with amplifications of some of these poems.

Therapy

Morning lights the walk-in closet
where our clothes hang like ghosts around us.
Bending off his groaning chair to tie
his shoe, my husband hears me say:
"I have a name for this work:
atmosphere altering. I try to taint
the air to make the house be happy."

His shoelace firm, my husband grins.
He knows about these things.
"The pundits call it *milieu therapy*."
I slide my drawer shut,
pull a sweater on, and deny.
"I don't do therapy. I stage
a scatter of good moments
for any one of my cronies
in any one day."

A GLOVE ON MY HEART

MIKE

Crazy as Hell

IN A COMMERCIAL West Seattle neighborhood, across the street from a steel mill, beside a huge new storage facility, nestles a lone frame house. One landscaped and green patch of land lies in the midst of motley, cemented chaos. Passing it on the bus, the unknowing observer, if he or she notices it at all, might guess this one house is occupied by holdouts who cling to their dwelling after all the other homeowners living here when the neighborhood was residential moved to pleasanter places. This 1930s-style single-family residence is only in one sense single-family now. It houses fifteen residents who are subject to the NIMBY syndrome—not in my back yard. Most families prefer living at some distance from the mentally ill. When the board of this licensed agency for the mentally ill bought this property in the early 70s, they were delighted that there was no organized or angry opposition to their plans to buy and remodel it to house a family of the mentally ill.

These mentally ill are in transition, being treated after and medicated for their psychotic breaks. They are in transition to whatever recovery and independent living is now possible for them. The agency's aim is to help them regain a sense of their own dignity and coping skills. To help them find jobs and learn some housekeeping and cooking capabilities before they move from this residence to their own living spaces is essential.

The house itself, set back from the street with a rock garden in front and parking lot beside it, has a trim and orderly air. Residents scarcely glance at the ugly steel mill down the hill and in front of their home when they go for their smokes to the broad front porch, which is hidden from the street by shrubbery. Do the clients regret this derelict scenery? Probably there is no resident so observant of his or her surroundings as to be depressed or energized—either way—by the location. Since the mentally ill often seem locked within themselves, their responses to their environment seem scarcely to extend beyond the front door. Neither beauty nor grime much matters: home is either safe or not. The agency aims to make every resident feel he or she belongs in this house.

The house's entry hall, its living room, its dining room, and kitchen are all furnished to make the place seem like a home rather than an institution. The TV is at the heart of the living room, and surrounding it are two sofas and three easy chairs. A huge picture of a sailing ship on one stuccoed white wall reminds those who glance at it that there is adventure in the world outside. It is the house's task to help clients be ready for the adventure of ordinary living again.

"Enrichment coordinator, that's what we'll call you, something like that," the agency's executive director had said to me when we met for lunch to discuss what I might do as a volunteer if I joined the staff for a year. "Writing groups, maybe a book club, the things you've done with other groups might work for us." Water glasses and cutlery sparkled around us at a small restaurant, and this was a lunch to brainstorm what I might do in my volunteer activities at this "live-in" mental health facility. Neither of us knew the first time we put our heads together in that genteel setting how unrealistic these initial ideas were. At the agency's annual meeting I had spoken with one of its alumni, a lawyer who said he would be interested in a writing group. That was the cue I hoped to build on. We did decide on a realistic working schedule, however: I would work four days a week, seven hours a day.

The sailing ship launched on a calm sea in the white-framed picture on our living room wall suggests to me the program supervisor's advice about activities to develop with the residents: "At least twice a week, try to take our clients out to a park, to the aquarium, to the science center, on a picnic or just out walking." This advice was the most useful anyone gave me. According to the house's program, if residents sign up to do at least three of the weekly chores around the house—dishes, cleaning, cooking dinner—they earn "privileges" and are eligible to go on outings. I found, however, that each week there were folks who needed to get out of the house as part of their socialization who hadn't actually done enough chores to earn a jaunt out. Their need and willingness to get out was what determined me to take them, rather than whether or not they had earned privileges. I found that holding strictly to rules didn't always help build a trusting relationship with a client, and I cared more about relationships than rules. The staff at the house, I found, either backed me or ignored me in my judgment calls when I bent the rules.

My first working day was a staff meeting day. I boarded the ferry across Puget Sound and rode the Seattle bus to work that day feeling tentative. I was not used to being with the mentally ill and thoughts of working with them left me a bit frightened. All I remember of the discussion at that meeting is about Mike, who appeared to persistently annoy the staff. He was gruff and confrontational. When he paced the halls, he pelted the staff with verbal insults. "These people all lie to me," was a phrase he repeated incessantly. Naïvely, that first morning I decided Mike was the man with whom to start.

At the staff meeting the program director counseled us, "Be patient. Until Mike's Clozaril kicks in there's probably nothing that's going to relieve us of his annoyance." I learned later that Clozaril is a powerful, slow-acting antipsychotic medication. The executive director spoke after the program director, with a suggestion that seemed aimed directly at me: "Find out what he likes to do, and do it with him. Maybe he likes to play cards." As the executive director's idea was thrown out on the agitated air of the room, I felt the yen for a card game. I needed an antidote to my uncertainty. Being new, I didn't notice that the idea of a card game seemed pretty lame to the rest of the staff. On this, my first day, I clutched at any idea as to what I could do.

So, after the staff meeting I took my sack lunch up to a dark nook of the second floor of the staff side of the house, and hid myself away to eat. To nestle on that sofa was a way to deal with my uncertainty, and it worked. I came out of hiding ready to confront Mike, or anyone else, with confidence. Downstairs, I found a group of residents gathered around the "med window" waiting for their medications. Mike was with them, arms folded stiffly across his chest, glaring. His jaw jerked as though he were adjusting some lump of stubborn food in his open mouth. He's a slight, middle-aged man with dark hair and a beard that sometimes sparkles with drool. I adopted a grave but upbeat tone. "You must be Mike. I'm Judy."

This stranger? How did she know his name? "You're old," he said.

"I know. But I like being old." I wasn't about to be cowed!

With dulled eyes, he studied my face. "I guess it ain't your fault you're old."

Did I detect the merest scrap of identification in his guess? "You know any card games?"

"Blackjack...rummy."

I settled on rummy, since I couldn't remember much about blackjack, and told him I'd find a deck of cards.

Finding cards turned out to be no small feat. Finally, a staff member rummaged in a drawer and found a deck and, because the August day was bright and breezy, we carried the cards out to the sunny side of the paved courtyard. I sat on a rickety wooden bench that also served as a playing surface. Mike sat opposite me in a rickety white plastic chair. It had been years since I'd played rummy, and I couldn't remember the rules. We used his. Not exact, but they worked. We played three or four games before another resident came along and asked to play. She knew different rules, and we got fouled up and quit. But I had accomplished my purpose: I had shown Mike that I had time for him, and I knew I liked him.

Mike most often nagged us with repeated phrases, and at first I fumbled some limp response. His most common question was "What do you want from me?"

One day he cornered the program director, who was walking through the dining room, and asked the same question of him.

"We want you to do something that'll make you proud of yourself." I didn't hear what Mike answered, I was so taken with the program director's catchy answer.

When next Mike asked me "What do you want from me?" I was ready.

"Do something that'll make you proud of yourself."

"Don' wanna. I been in plenty places that want me to be proud of myself. Don' wanna."

So much for that one. I readied a different answer for the next time. "We just want you to be happy!" That one worked for a couple of months: when I used it, Mike grinned and shut up.

It began to be very clear what Mike wanted of me. Each day he tossed out the name of a place and asked if I'd go there with him: Oklahoma City…Kelso…Enumclaw. Each time I found some excuse. They were all too far away. "You've got a lot on the ball, I wish I could go home with you," he said one day. That was the toughest one. Although I tried, I couldn't seem to drum up a gentle rejection!

That year Tom was the man who swept the floors, fixed the broken appliances, cleaned all three bathrooms, and mopped regularly. His upbeat, steady manner was almost more important to our residents than the thorough and essential cleaning job he did. About my second month in the house, he took a week's vacation. By the time he'd been gone only two days the dining room floor was despicably coffee-stained and grungy. I decided to try to get someone to mop it. If I failed, I'd do it myself. Mike was a coffee drinker. (We provided ground coffee—decaffeinated only—and the residents brewed it for themselves in a communal pot.) Mike never made coffee himself, but on his pacing travels through the dining room he often frowned at the machine, and when it had coffee, he liked to pour some for himself. He couldn't be bothered to get himself a clean cup. He grabbed the first receptacle he found, clean or not. When he had poured it, he paced about drinking it, generously sloshing it over the floor. On one of his perpetual jaunts upstairs, I passed him with coffee stains on his shirt front. "What about it? Would you like to help me mop the floor?" I asked.

"Naa. Don' wanna."

I continued down the stairs, raided the cleaning closet, pulled out the mop bucket on wheels, and was piling the chairs on top of the dining room table when Mike appeared. "I'll do it," and he grabbed the mop and squeezed the water from it into the mop bucket as he'd seen Tom do. Mop ready, he swished it over the coffee stains to remove them. They almost disappeared. When the mop had been pushed around in several places the floor was puddled and cleaner.

I fell to using a kind of blather when speaking with Mike. My talk was so zany that sometimes I could hardly believe it was I speaking with him. I mimicked him, joshed him, let him know I disbelieved his claims. The poem "The Devil" is an illustration.

The Devil

Your hair is parted today
but drool beads your sandy beard.
You put two fingers to your head
make horns, then point at me.
Your toothless grin says:
"You've got the devil in you."

I put fingers to my forehead,
fire back. You retreat:
"Naw, Satan's not really
In you, but he's plenty in the world."
I cock my head: "You mean
    everyone sins but you and me?"
You nod your head, agree.

Next time I'll take a finger,
circle my head in a halo,
point at you, and make you
into a swaggering angel!

The road with Mike was bumpy. His saner days didn't come one after the other. I'd think we were ahead, and he'd do something that would toss me back. Appearing to resist the sitting position, he either paced or lay on his bed, and seldom sat to do anything, especially eat. One day at the lunch table, when everyone else was spooning fruited yogurt from individual cups, he passed the table, and when I asked him, he said he'd like a yogurt. I rushed to the fridge to get one for him before someone else—a readier eater than he—got the last one. Pulling the small container out I dropped it, and it rolled under the fridge. "Mike, come help." I called. He came, dropped to his knees, and peered under the refrigerator. I dropped to my knees too, and the two of us found ourselves kneeling on our prayer bones to see under the fridge. He reached under, rolled out the container, and stood again. When we were both on our feet, he hugged me. "I love you," he said.

"I love you, too," I shot back, wondering if I was supposed to share that particular truth with him.

The next day Mike's warmth had vanished. The house had some new mattress pads. I knew his pad had disappeared, having seen him lying on the bare plastic of his mattress. No sheet. I took a pad to his room, knocked on his door, and asked if he would please put the pad on his bed. "Don' wanna. Go to hell," he said.

"But you'll like your bed so much better if it's softer," I pleaded.

"Don' wan' it. Go to hell!"

With the commotion his roommate had risen. "I want it! Put it on my bed," Hugo piped, and Hugo got the mattress pad.

Some days Mike talked my ear off—almost all random thoughts. As he walked past me, he would repeat certain phrases. Things like "I got relatives in Port Townsend." Another: "My aunt in Port Townsend is sick. Six months ago she had a heart attack, a stroke. I wanna call my aunt in Port Townsend." I didn't know how to respond to this request, but the program director heard it in passing. "Can you wait until Saturday, when your case manager will help you? If your aunt were here she'd tell you to wipe the slobber off your beard." Sheepishly Mike lifted a shaking hand mapped with veins and touched his beard, but did not rid it of drool. The next time he walked through the dining room he had a new phrase: "Jesus died on the cross."

Since Mike spoke of religious faith, I used his faith to help build

Place Your Bets

This morning you offer to shake on it.
"Five bucks my folks are in heaven."
"I'll bet on that! But how will we find out?"
You grin. "I'm smart, aren't I?"

Then: "Ya know the Sermon on the Mount?"
"Blessed are the meek..." I begin.
"For they shall inherit the Earth," you answer.
"Blessed are those who hunger and thirst after righteousness,"
"For they shall be filled."
You know it. "I'm smart, aren't I?"

"They're gonna chop my head off, Gramma."
"But what would we do with it?" I ask.
That stumps you.

a relationship with him. Clearly, at some time he had attended church regularly—often enough to learn a number of hymns and biblical passages. But he did not appear to attend any religious service now. Still, his faith seemed to preoccupy his thoughts and sometimes give him assurance, as the poem on the facing page suggests.

One day his phrase was "Wouldn't you love to see Jesus?" and my glib answer was "Sure, I'd love to see Jesus." Nothing more. However, about the sixth time he asked me, I was weary. I looked at him, searching his face, and said, "Sure I would. And sometimes I think I see Jesus right in your face."

It worked. He grinned and said no more. The next morning he had a new greeting when I arrived: "Well, if it isn't Mary Magdalene."

Later that day his phrase was again: "I'm smart, aren't I?"

It was important to have an answer when Mike asked, as he did almost every day, "What do you want from me?" After several months of saying "We just want you to be happy," I hit on a new quip. "I want a song." That bit of play meant that Mike, unfailingly, began to sing for me. He knew a variety of songs: "I Came to the Garden Alone," "Joshua Fit the Battle of Jericho," and countless other folk songs. But never would he sing out loud. His tune was always mumbled under his breath, but he made sure I got the words, singing them to me as if they were private, for me alone.

The high point of my year with Mike came when I took him for a medical appointment. Our medical coordinator found a suspicious spot on Mike's chest, and anticipating he would need a biopsy, made an appointment at the local university hospital. Since the biopsy appointment turned out to be at a time when Mike's case manager was not available, I volunteered to take him.

"They're gonna kill me, Gramma," Mike said as we headed to the clinic in the house's van. By this time I'd become Gramma to him. I sensed that he might be more frightened than he was letting on. I knew I was frightened. His case manager had warned me that he'd be nervous and would need reassurance, and suggested I buy him a Coke. Mike had not, however, been too frightened to get in the van and go.

"They can't kill you. You're some kind of angel." I stared

straight ahead at the road. He said nothing. I thought I felt him grin.

We were traveling on the crowded freeway just at noon, and I turned off to take a back route. It took longer to reach the hospital, but it gave both of us time to treat our prospects more casually.

"They lie to me," Mike mused.

"Who lies to you? If you're an angel they can't lie to you." Being wary myself, I fought his delusions as I usually did not. Usually I let his crazy ideas wash over me, and brushed them off as if they weren't worth commenting on. If his fears now had any shred of truth to them, I wanted to be as zany as I knew how to be!

We arrived at the clinic late, but the doctor was running behind. They told us it would be a half-hour. The moment for the Coke! I bought us each a Coke—I don't like Coke—and we went out onto a hospital balcony to enjoy the view while we drank. When we returned to the clinic we were told it would be another half-hour. What to do? I've said Mike seldom sits down, but in this hospital waiting room he was willing to sit side by side with me on the clinic's chairs and speak to me in a quiet voice, as if we were normal people.

Mike decided he was hungry. "I got eighty thousand dollars. I want Chinese food, Gramma."

"Maybe when we get back we can go for Chinese food." Neither of us knew when we'd get back to the house. I knew it might be well past the end of my shift, and I wouldn't want to hang around to go for Chinese food.

As we sat waiting, Mike spouted his regular phrases. "I'm smart, aren't I?" and "My mom's in heaven, Gramma." The frequency and variety of his phrases reflected his nervousness. I was still nervous too. A nurse came out to the waiting room with some questions for us. She too was jumpy, and I guessed she knew something of Mike's mental health history.

At last the same nurse emerged again and directed us to a small examining room. She seemed relieved when I asked to accompany Mike. I had been told he was not very good at giving his medical history and that I might need to fill in where he left out key items. Indeed, the only information he offered this mousy woman was that he'd been taking medication for his mental illness for fifteen years. In the papers I'd brought I had more information, and offered the pertinent parts of it. After telling us it might be a while until the doctor came in, the nurse left. I flashed a quick smile at Mike, who now sat three feet away from me wearing a white hospital gown instead of a shirt. He began to sing: "We gotta stop, my God yes, stop killing one another." Now he sensed I needed calming. The grin on his face made me want to lean over and hug him.

Another long wait. At last the doctor came in, asked only a few questions, examined the suspicious spot, and decided he would like to cut a piece of Mike's flesh for a biopsy. Tentative, the doctor began to describe what he wanted to do. He needed Mike's permission to perform the surgery required for a biopsy, and getting permission from a mental patient was not a familiar task to him. His request lacked punch; his tone made it sound as if he'd be relieved if Mike refused. Finally I broke in. "Lets do it, huh?"

"Yeah," Mike grunted. I hoped the doctor's knife would be sharper and quicker than his words.

The hospital needed Mike's signature on a release form, and the same nurse appeared to finesse it. Mike gave her no trouble and she left us, again clearly relieved, with the necessary forms in hand. Mike was beginning to have fun. He sang the same song again. "We gotta stop, my God yes...stop killing one another." After some fifteen minutes, however, he appeared to be ready to rip the gown off and get out of the tiny room. "I wanna eat Chinese food, Gramma."

Mike's request to use the restroom ended our wait. When he graduated from the restroom to the procedure room instead of going back to the tiny examining room, it was my turn to be relieved. Mike, by contrast, was warming up to this adventure. He happily climbed onto the procedure room table.

A second nurse arrived and asked what kind of music Mike liked. "Elvis," he said. No luck; they didn't have Elvis. "Elton John?" he asked. They didn't have him either.

"What do you think of Sting?"

"What's that?" The nurse gave up trying to find music to please him, and Mike began to sing on his own. "Morning has broken...."

I joined him. "...like the first morning." Neither of us knew more words.

This new nurse said she had sung this Cat Stevens song twenty years ago at her eighth-grade graduation, and she leapt into song with us.

The three of us were singing when the doctor came to numb the suspicious spot with a needle.

"Is that sore?" he asked, again tentative.

"I can hack it. Can I sing a song?"

The doctor was preoccupied with the incision he made, and when he made no answer Mike's soft singing voice cut through the silence. He was still singing as the doctor sutured the wound. "Joy to the fishes in the deep blue sea, joy to you and me." Mike's voice cheered all four of us.

The doctor finished, said goodbye, and disappeared. The nurse instructed me about how to keep the wound clean as if Mike were my child. "Two weeks and the stitches come out." Mike climbed off the table and we straggled triumphant from the hospital to the van. Traveling home, Mike was sober and spoke very little. "I want Chinese food, Gramma."

Two hours later—on Mike's ten dollars—we went for Chinese food. Seeing us leave, two of Mike's housemates who'd already eaten dinner asked to join us. Glad for the company, even if they would only watch us eat, we agreed to take them. These two men liked Mike. He liked them.

Careful to stay under budget, I ordered egg foo yung for myself, and chop suey for Mike when he indicated that's what he wanted. Mike gobbled two of my three egg foo yung patties, and most of his chop suey. The bill was over ten dollars when our two guests were charged a "service fee" for their water. I forked out happily. It was a celebration!

Two weeks later we learned that the biopsy had tested negative. Still, I'm glad this event happened. Now when Mike speaks, as he so frequently does, about getting out of the house, I can make my stock answer with less zaniness and more meaning. "What would we do if you left us? We want you here!" Mike regularly transforms me. He's become a fixture at the house, and I think the entire staff knows the place would not seem right without him.

After I finished full-time work at the house, I continued to go back each Tuesday to fill in during staff meetings. One Tuesday morning as I came into the house Mike was in the doorway.

"Where you been?" he asked, stretching his arms out wide and enfolding me.

"How you been?" I murmured into his beard.

"Crazy as hell," he said.

"Fiddle-faddle," I said. After that, Mike often called me "Fiddle Faddle."

WILLIAM

The Good That I Would, I Do Not

IT WAS WHILE working with William, instructing him how to clean his bathroom, that I conceived the title for this book. I remembered that when doing work that carries a risk of contamination, it is advisable to wear protective gloves. In that same session it struck me that when working with the mentally ill, encouraging them to change, to behave in more "acceptable" ways, there is the danger of becoming too much involved. One needs a protective glove over one's heart. I found I could express this idea in poetry better than in prose, and the poem appears on the opposite page.

Hearing staff talk in the house about how "ill" someone was often gave me a jolt. It shocked me to observe the contrast between the professional staff's more informed assessment of a person's mental state and my gut feeling. I was, after all, a volunteer. I had little training in the field of mental illness. Through a kind of psychological osmosis I'd gleaned a patchy knowledge from my husband. I had nothing more than my intuition to guide me, and I could never be sure of my own intuition. Often I judged a person to be healthier than the staff said he was. Such contrasts made me wary, but I let my own experience guide my actions. I wanted to be upbeat. I sensed that if I dealt with a person with even a scrap of criticism or fear, it would be harder to build a trusting relationship.

William, a young man with a smiling, puffy face, was a conundrum for me. I could never quite understand how such a pink blimp of a guy, assessed by the staff as so sick, could be so likeable. While sitting at the dining room table one morning soon after I began work at the house, I heard a brash male voice speaking behind me in the telephone alcove. This man sounded more on top

A Glove on My Heart

The man on the floor below complains
he smells your bathroom.
As if aid is your right, you ask
for help to clean it.
No one comes. You call me
to come and see how bad it is.

I come, I see, I thank God
age mutes my sense of smell.
"For all such dirty jobs you
should wear protective gloves,"
I croon. You protest
and both of us forget the gloves.

I bring Lysol, instruct. "Pick
up the toilet brush, swish it,
use it hard in the toilet."
You function, give yourself praise.
"See, I can do it," until I shake a
finger at a pile of filthy
rags beneath the sink.
"I can't bend down," you say.
"You're going to have to," I say.
You bend, you creak, you scrub
the spotted wash-bowl,
sponge-mop the smelly floor
till even I can smell the clean
and you're too tuckered to be proud.

As I put on my coat to go
you vow you'll douse your dirt
with Lysol every Thursday.
Promises come easy, I observe,
and pull a glove onto my heart
to keep from too much hope for you.

Next week, I'm almost certain,
you'll forget to clean.

of things, more sane, than I was beginning to expect of any of his housemates. When the young man appeared in the dining room I introduced myself. His name was William, and somehow his manner indicated that it mattered for him to meet me. This was aplomb. I liked him right off. It was only later, when I could resist letting such knowledge influence me, that I learned the grim details of his history.

Our friendship—William's and mine—was cemented initially by an excursion we took together to take the test for a food handler's permit. Our house prided itself on insisting that, as part of their training for more independent living, our residents plan and help cook their own meals. In order to cook in the kitchen, however, staff and residents both had to pass the food handler's permit test. While William and I rode downtown together on the bus he told me about his school experience. He told me proudly that his teachers had told him he had a better than average IQ. We got off the bus several blocks from the public health building where the test was administered. As we walked there I first observed that William walked with a marked limp.

"What happened that you limp so?" I asked.

He continued to lurch along, pants low on his hips and cuffs dragging on the ground before he said, "I jumped off a bridge. I'm here by the grace of God." I could make no comment. I fell in behind him and noticed the pink blush of his behind showing above his waist band.

"I think a belt might help keep your pants from dragging behind your heels," I said.

"Gotta get one, don't have one," he said.

When we reached the office where the test was administered, William asked for fifteen more minutes to study the food handler's pamphlet before he took the multiple-choice test. Good idea! I followed his lead and took more time to study too, and William continued to call the shots. When he was ready we took the test. I worked away, thinking it was no breeze, and was startled when William stepped up to the desk and turned in his test. How could he have answered all the questions so rapidly? The man behind the desk had already declared him "passed" by the time I finished. William had missed four questions, the maximum he could miss and still pass the test. It took me longer, but I missed only one.

William forever dreamed of food. When we left the testing office in a celebratory mood, he said he was hungry. It was too early in my career at the house for me to know the procedure for treats for the clients when we were out, so I bought him something to eat with my own money. He gobbled the sandwich we found at a sidewalk stand, and we returned to the house on the bus, both of us sporting a triumphant air. My sense of triumph was for William. He had conquered the test, and had grandiose plans for what he would cook at the house now that he had passed. My gut told me, "Beware. You're beginning to feel too close to a client. He might let you down."

My come uppance came the following day. William did nothing but sleep on the living room sofa all morning. So much for "progress." Improvements he made in his life were going to have to overcome his sloth. Did his mental illness exacerbate his inertia? Probably. Still, that was no reason to think he would never take better care of himself. Surely the same principle must apply to William that I saw in all human growth. *Expecting* better behavior was part of what encouraged it.

I continued to wonder whether William was as mentally ill as he was rumored to be. When he was up and about the house he was full of ideas and dreams. He also had friends at his church with whom he fraternized and even went on retreats. I did notice he tended to "use" his friends, and that his housemates didn't seem to like him. The house staff who had known him over the years thought of him as a "Clozaril" miracle since he functioned so much better now than when they first knew him.

A game of monopoly? William was always up for that. He liked to be the banker, and when I landed on St. James Place, he could tell me without looking whether it was already sold and what the rent was. In between, he often looked up and told me my glasses needed lifting. He added and subtracted accurately, all in his head. He bought property as if he owned all the money in the bank, and then when he discovered he had no more money he mortgaged his property at a furious rate to buy more. Working this way, he was either a huge winner or, in one fell swoop, he lost. Out of the game! He liked to win, but he lost cheerfully. I never saw him morose.

When the exhibit "Leonardo Lives" opened at the Seattle Art Museum, I decided to take several of the people from the house who I thought would enjoy it to see it one by one. I figured the hands-on display of some of Leonardo da Vinci's experiments would particularly appeal to several of our male clients. But the trips were not stellar successes. None of my companions showed much enthusiasm for the hands-on room. Was it because they sensed the enormity of Leonardo's curiosity and imagination, in contrast with their own? Still, William asked to go after each of the others came back and reported what he had seen.

"You don't want your behind to show at the Art Museum, do you? You'll have to wear a belt," I warned. William somehow acquired a belt, and asked for help threading it through the loops in his pants. When we arrived at the museum William had a surprise for me. He used his manipulative skills, asked for a wheelchair, obtained one, and asked me to wheel him about the exhibit. Wheeling the handicapped was a new experience for me. I enjoyed proving my stamina, and William relished his dependent state. The models of hands-on experiments, when we bucked the crowds into that room, didn't intrigue William; but he was fascinated when I pushed him up to a computer where he could read replicas of Leonardo's handwritten accounts of his experiments and theories. William was the only person I took who said he'd like to go back so he could read more of the Codex Leicester. Whether his curiosity was genuine or not, he further endeared himself to me by expressing it openly.

The surest sign of William's progress came when the staff at the house decided he was ready for independent living and arranged for him to move to a house the agency rented two doors away from the main house. The move meant he would need to return to the med window at the main house each day for his medications, but he could manage his own finances, do his own grocery shopping, cook his own meals, and do his own laundry and cleaning. At the main house everyone does their own laundry, and the way William kept his clothes hardly boded well for the way he would manage other hygiene and cooking skills. Still, it boosted his morale to start living on his own. He needed the chance to show he was capable of growth. He liked his small house, even though there was no housemate. (He was promised he would get a housemate soon.) After all, he could consider himself as having gained a certain amount of independence.

One day while visiting William I caught a glimpse of his bedroom. The room was so covered with clutter that it was impossible to see an inch of the room's cherished fir-wood floor. Did he intend to put the room in order? He said he wanted to. I knew William wanted to do a host of good things, but he lacked the will to actually do them. We set a date for the following Monday to begin working together on organizing his books, his papers, and his clothing. Our plan was to assign all his "stuff" to some kind of appropriate place to be kept.

On the following Monday he called to stall. A friend at his church would have made him a tall shelf by Friday, so why didn't we put our work off? I went to his house anyway, figuring there'd be other work. Indeed, the bedroom work overwhelmed without a shelf, but the kitchen also needed to be cleared of its clutter. I offered to help William cook a dinner, with recipes from his cookbook, if he would choose a recipe, wash the dishes, and sweep the floor. Not wanting to stand over him like a slave driver while he worked, I did small jobs that would not occur to him, like scrubbing the catsup splatters off the cupboards. When he started to wash the dishes, I observed that he appeared to have no idea how to draw water, get soap suds, and get dishes clean. I showed him and, halfhearted though he was, he began. I left him working alone to go back to the main house and monitor lunch-making there.

When I returned an hour later William was watching television, having finished most of the dishes. A pile of sand and bits of food remained on the floor to be swept into the dust pan, which he claimed he couldn't find. We found a flat piece of paper, swept the litter onto it, found his cookbook under a pile of dirty underwear, and I showed him how to sauté pork chops. We improvised a "pizza" sauce to smother them while they cooked.

The next day William was full of enthusiasm for his own cooking. "The chops were great. Your glasses needed lifting. I'd like to make those chops again."

By the following Friday his friend had delivered the bookshelf, and we spent two hours in the morning and two hours in the afternoon putting things onto the shelves. While we worked William played gospel songs on a new tape player he had bought himself in honor of his new house. What kind of music did I like? One song we heard had words that went, "Ev'ry day with Jesus is sweeter than the day before."

"I remember that one from my childhood Sunday school days," I told him. When we quit that day the floor was still littered with clothing and papers waiting to "get organized." I suggested he finish the job, but I knew he probably wouldn't. He did say he wanted to, though.

Knowing that William was short on determination and long on fantasy, one day I asked him how his Christian faith could help him get his life turned around so that he actually did some of the things he said he wanted to do. He didn't seem to get my question, so I changed my tack and amazed myself with the language I used. "Could Jesus help you get your daily living on a cleaner foot?" It was a very long time before he answered, so long I thought he was nonplussed and that I shouldn't have asked. Then, quite suddenly, he said "You pray to God, and then you take the initiative." Now it was my turn to be nonplussed. I hadn't expected this kind of innate wisdom. I went on to remind him that Paul had used the phrase, "The good that I would, I do not."

"Paul was speaking of the human condition," I said. "Most of us are dreamers. We want all kinds of good things, but to overcome our inertia, to actually take the steps to grow into the place we want to be, is something else. You're right. Prayer can give us the will, but we have to lift our hands, move our feet, act—take the initiative!"

I left William that day regretfully. I had found it hard to hear him mouth the words of faith without seeing him practice that faith, and I had succumbed to preaching. Why couldn't I keep my mouth shut? Be content with the good you've seen, I told myself. For William, I observed, faith does a lot. It helps him plug the hole in his soul. I shouldn't ask his faith to help him "take the initiative."

On a day about six weeks after his move William telephoned me one morning.

"Hey, can you come over?"

"Maybe. What you have in mind?"

"The guy downstairs says he can smell my bathroom."

"What are you going to do about it?"

"I guess I gotta clean it, but I don't know how."

"So you want me to show you? I'm not up for cleaning someone else's bathroom, but...I'll come and bring Lysol, and show you."

He cleaned the bathroom, and the following day I helped him make a chart listing all the household chores that needed regular attention. The reward I offered was a trip to the funky café down the street for a treat. I told him that on the weeks when there were checks in all the blanks we'd go to the café. We had made the chart and I had returned to the house when our medical coordinator got a phone call. William had thrown up and needed help. Watching our doctor go off to check on him, I speculated: Was it the mere thought of all the work the chores involved that had made William ill?

William's illness lingered for four days. I went to visit him that Friday afternoon and found him lounging on the davenport watching TV. He accepted my offer to go to the library and get video tapes for him. At other times when I had taken William with others to the library to check out whatever he chose, he had sometimes chosen historical videos. He liked documentary accounts of China's revolution or the American Civil War. He was also one of the few clients in the house who had ever expressed interest in watching the news on TV. Encouraging his natural curiosity made it more fun to chat with him.

William watched television and longed to be in love. Once he asked for my help in writing a letter to a girl he had known when he was a boy. He called me in to where he was sitting at a computer and asked me to help him phrase the letter so that she would answer it. What he hoped for was an actual correspondence with this woman of his fantasy. When we had composed the letter it turned out he hadn't a clue how to find her address.

William *was* more lovable when he was in love. One summer day he approached me to tell me in a low squeal that he wanted to talk to me. I suggested we go to the other porch, away from the crowd, and when he took my arm to steer me there I sensed excitement in his movements. Having seated ourselves, he in a plastic chair that he could just barely squeeze into, I beside him, he looked at me and bleated, "What do you *do* when you're away from your husband? How do you stand it?"

"You're in love!" I guessed.

"She's gone to Oklahoma City. But she's coming back." His moon face was aglow.

"Where'd you meet her?"

"Right here." He named a huge young woman who had recently been a guest in our guest room, because the house offered her respite from her mental crisis as it often does temporarily for other mentally ill people. I remember her for two phrases: "Ya gotta let Jesus be in charge," and "That's why I like teddy bears, they look so much like Jesus."

"Love's great. I hope it works for you," I told William.

Afterwards, thinking about them, I decided these two persons had two things in common: Being large, and being "Jesus freaks."

I remembered, too, that William looked like a teddy bear!

The Power of a Pill

You're sick. Four days and you still
do nothing but watch the boob tube.
When I visit, you say, "Lots of people
praying for me." I guess you mean,
"You may not care, but others do."

I have no pills to offer.
Instead I clean a spot on the floor
your roommate blames on puke.
S.O.S. takes it. While I scour you lunge
to the commode for raucous heaves you hope
I hear. Between each retch you yell
out the open door: "Gotta see a doctor!"

Our house doctor shuns pills,
declares, "It simply has to run
its course." More stubborn than
sick, you rise, take yourself
on the bus to a clinic,
persuade the doctor there to
give you a magic pill, and
afterward, get well!

SAMANTHA

The Way To Do Is To Be

SAMANTHA WILL want all the time she can get from you," the program director warned me in our first training session. I sensed he was saying, "Don't let Samantha suck up any more of your time than you want her to." What neither he nor I recognized at that point was that I would *need* to give time to Samantha. My work was such that unless I could get someone to do something with me, I wasn't accomplishing anything. Many mornings when I came into the house everyone else was in bed, but Samantha was up and ready to do whatever I suggested. Often she had her own ideas.

If the kitchen sink was full of egg-spattered dishes and greasy frying pans and the chore chart was blank with no one's name on it on that particular morning, Samantha could always be persuaded to work with me to clean it up. I worked only until she was well started, then pulled out, leaving her to a plodding finish. Music blared from a small radio while she worked putting away the food, rinsing the dishes, loading the dish washer, and wiping the counters. Slow strokes made her particularly thorough at wiping the counters. She always wanted to help when we cooked something special, although she didn't do any task without being told to and needed careful instruction at each phase of any operation.

A third person was needed when William and I wanted to play monopoly. William's erratic popularity in the house meant he could not easily attract other players, but Samantha was always a ready candidate. She needed shepherding, coaching through the game, but she *was* a third player. William was a born coach, and Samantha was one of the few who tolerated his bossy direction.

Samantha: "I don't understand. What's a mortgage?"

William: "It's the way you get the money you need." Stopping for nothing, William would grab several of her properties, read the amount she would earn when she mortgaged them, and hand her the cash from the bank.

Samantha: "I don't understand."

William: "That's okay, Samantha, you did it."

One time William coached Samantha into buying and placing hotels on Boardwalk and Park Place. Then he landed on Park Place and had to give her everything he owned.

William: "I'm out of the game."

Samantha: "I don't understand."

William, cooing: "That's okay, Samantha, you're winning."

In that particular game I longed to help Samantha sustain her triumph. But William couldn't coach her into better luck. I tried, but I started too late, and couldn't jimmy the game around so I would lose.

Samantha was always game to go to the library. When she borrowed children's books to read, she enjoyed looking at the pictures, and she particularly enjoyed books with math puzzles. She worked forever at those puzzles, with little success. Once, when we began to read together a book she had chosen, she read the first paragraph over and over aloud. "I don't understand. Will you explain it?"

"It means...." When I tried to translate the meaning into simpler language she continued with her "I don't understand" and reread the same paragraph aloud.

Happily, she never failed to understand when she talked about buying something she wanted, like a coat. Those were the times she sparkled with childlike vivacity. At the beginning of October she hatched an enthusiastic plan to make a fairy queen costume for Halloween. Her talk was just that, however: talk. It didn't seem to bother her that her dream of regal glory got pared down for her actual Halloween costume to a colored paper crown with sparkles pasted on it. She thought about and wanted to do countless things, but the moment she spoke of a wish, it seemed to vanish like water poured into other water. Without major help, she could not sustain the plans she made.

When we went together one day to get her a haircut, the highlight of the trip was going to Bartell's to pick out a chocolate bar with the money she had left. I disliked shopping with her, however, because my own buying habits are practical, and she adored buying frivolously. Once we embarked on an extensive shopping search for a dress she said she wanted to wear to church. (I hadn't been aware she went to church.) In about the fourth store we went into, where she tried on many dresses, she chose a white dress with lace on it. About a week later, when I knocked on her door one morning, I found her wearing the dress as a nightgown.

More than any other of our residents, Samantha seemed a pawn of the mental health system—a victim of the state's bureaucracy. Our house was the only home she knew. But one day her case manager, finding no progress in Samantha's charts (we suspected she was both developmentally disabled and mentally ill), felt compelled to do what the state required: transfer Samantha to a congregate care facility. We needed to find a place whose charter didn't include preparing clients for more independent living and who would not charge the state as much for her room and board. Our house had a different mission: to see if our residents could learn to live more independently. In short, Samantha had failed that test. If she had had a family supporting her the system might not have jerked her around so readily. But she had no parents, nor even a memory of parents. She spoke of a grandmother, but she couldn't tell me how old she had been when her grandmother was in her life. She asked me once to help her locate a former foster mother so that she could deliver a Christmas present to her. We tried the only phone number she could dig up, and it had been disconnected. The poem on the following page describes how much I realized I would miss Samantha when she had gone.

If left to eat only the foods she chose, Samantha filled up on junk food. This meant that bowel regularity was one of her problems. Our medical coordinator suggested she eat limited quantities of dairy products, particularly cheese. Since her favorite food was packaged macaroni and cheese, this was hard. Someone decided that popcorn binds as well, and she was forbidden to have popcorn. For both selfish and sympathetic reasons I could be persuaded to enter into a conspiracy with Samantha. She would sneak a bag of popcorn to microwave at times when we were both restless. Then we became sneaks, eating our popcorn when no one was about and shoving it beneath the table when someone who might enforce the popcorn ban happened along.

Leavetaking

They say you'll leave the house
next week, move to a CCF.
I ask what that means, and they say,
"Congregate Care Facility."
"Is that a step up?"
"No, a step down.
It saves the state's money
since we can do no more for her."

There's no one I'll miss more.
Who will be game for any
thing I try, insist at every step
"I just don't understand."
I ignore your pleas for help,
and you accept my silence.
It's as if some inner worm
gnaws gently at your brain.

You can't recall my name, but
there's no one I'll miss more.
Who'll make popcorn just to
share with me? Who'll give me lollipops
that last my whole ride home?

Playing at conspiracy enlivened Samantha. Much of the time when she was in the house with nothing to do I found her dozing in the living room like a hunched, cold cormorant, her black hair feathered and hanging about her face.

The timing of Samantha's move turned out to be particularly sad. Because the system had no regard for its charges' feelings, it happened that Samantha was to make the move out of the house just three days before Christmas. Our program supervisor, however, recognized how involved Samantha was in anticipating Christmas in the house. She spent hours thinking about and listing the presents she would buy for the people she cared about. The present she got me went against her frivolous inclinations. It was a fuzzy circle for my car's steering wheel, to keep my hands warm when I drove. She was so pleased with it that she insisted I open it on the first morning I came to the house after she bought it, so that she could watch my face as I did so.

Once the staff knew that Samantha was so involved with Christmas and gift-giving in the house, an alternative plan was made for her move. The move would go ahead, but she would come back early Christmas morning to spend the day with her friends. The house engaged a taxi to provide transportation, and Samantha was at the heart of the gift exchange in the house she called home.

After she was moved to the congregate care facility (CCF), Samantha's medications continued to require that her blood be checked weekly, and for this the system worked in her favor. A public access bus brought her back each week to have her blood tested along with her former housemates who needed similar checks. On those days she stayed around to go on outings or participate in whatever activity was planned for that day.

One morning, while I walked down the hill from my bus stop, an aid car passed me, sirens blasting. When I reached the house I found the same car parked outside, and I was told that Samantha was stretched out on the office floor. She had vomited a green fluid while coming to the house and passed out when she arrived. When she was taken for diagnosis, nothing could be found except possibly some fault in her liver. Of course I was concerned about Samantha and any suffering she was experiencing. At the same time, when I thought about the quality of the life I had observed in her, I had a question that is expressed in the poem on the following page.

A Fault in the Liver

They've moved you.
I've heard you stay in bed all day.
Here, you rose and sat head bowed
till spirit swirling near you
nudged you out of lethargy.

Forever ready to buy clothes,
you chose a white dress for church
and wore it for a nightgown.
Any game you play you hedge
by claiming "I don't understand,"
Still…willful, you hang in.

For your weekly blood draw
A bus brings you back to us.
One day when I arrive an ambulance
lurks beside our house. Inside you
lie on the office floor, where
a puzzled staff hovers.
Tests discover your liver's faulty.
I think of all your blanks.
You who love to try puzzles you never can complete.
You who clean counters for pleasure.
Might it not be best, I wonder,
if your liver takes you young?

Today the bus brings you back again.
I open the door, come in, and
from your usual droop you lift your head.
Your face lights up. You
have smiled at me to say with Lao Tsu
"The way to do is to be."

This young woman's life was fraught with things she tried to do but could not. But no vain efforts could defeat her. Again and again she tried to paint by number, cook, read, type, do math. This persistence—a kind of courage to be—endeared her to me, and those she lived with counted on her steadiness.

By a fluke, the system closed the congregate care facility where we had placed Samantha, and suddenly she was back home with us. Six other clients who were left homeless after the closure came to our house as well. I was delighted to have Samantha back. Again I had an ever-ready person with whom to do things: go on outings, play games, clean the kitchen, and especially go swimming with a group that had just begun to go swimming each week.

The word was, however, that Samantha was with us only temporarily. Her new classification meant that we were required to find another CCF for her. Eager to get her into a home where she'd be happy, I made inquiries at a group home near our home, even though it was in a different county. I found that they would accept her at this facility and that I could continue my interest in her by taking her on excursions and doing things with her.

Our agency piled all her stuff into our van and moved her. She seemed happy as she settled into the new home, where she had a private room. They liked her. But the system failed her again. When her new home found that the state mental health system would not approve her placement, she was shunted right back to us. By this time another client had been moved into her old room, so we had to put Samantha in a small apartment just across the driveway from the house. She could, however, participate in the house's activities, and she thought she had returned home, if only temporarily.

The day I came to the house and found her back, it was my turn to break into a broad smile. To welcome Samantha back I suggested she go swimming with the group. To celebrate, we leaped twenty jumps up in the pool holding hands. She had that same sparkle, but her mental illness was no better and no worse than the day I first met her. The poem "To Swim Is To Enter Heaven," on the following page, describes her moods in the swimming pool.

To Swim Is To Enter Heaven

Each swimming Tuesday I invade
your room to wake you, shake
your shoulder, make you groan.

Later you appear, swim suit on
beneath your clothes, so hip to go
you forget to take your meds.

The pool transforms your mood.
You grin, grab hands, circle,
dance. From ten leaps up
you never do come down.

Today I caught you playing ring-a-rosy,
holding hands with two strange men.
One haggard, gentle man stuck
for twenty water-sparkling jumps.

Another day you'll go, hang back.
To penetrate that pool will be like
plunging into hell.

After I'd worked at the home about three weeks, I described my work to a friend as being with "loonies." Samantha was one of those whom I dubbed, playfully, loony—to myself as well as in my stories about my work. But after I'd used the word many times, I had an insight described in the poem "To You, Our Client."

As fondly as I might think of people, if I called them loony they lost a chunk of their dignity not only in other people's perceptions, but in my own conception of them. I seldom use the word now.

To You Our Client, with Respect

You're loony, I'm loony.
The loony in you
brings out the zany in me,
and you become my crony.
I caught myself calling you loony
this morning, and I want to say I'm sorry.
I meant it fondly but
the person I spoke to
understood the word
like lunatic.

I think of loony like
the graceful water bird:
crisscrossed feathers,
a haunting call. The white ring
a loon wears around its neck
keeps it captive to its nature.
A zany brain holds you hostage.
When I hear a loon's night cry,
I am drawn to yearn.

When I call you loony
I hope you know
I yearn with you.

PETER AND SIMON

How Can I Keep from Singing?

PETER

WHEN SOMEONE is both mentally ill and uncertain of English, theirs is a rocky path to coping. For brief interviews with a psychiatrist, an interpreter can be hired. But day to day our house staff was left to find ways to ensure two-way communication with non-native English speakers. This means we were frequently unsure we understood or were understood.

Peter's family had immigrated to the United States from Asia some five years ago. When our family lived in Turkey I taught English as a second language to Turks, so when I learned there was a resident who was eager for English lessons, I volunteered. My hunch was that language lessons could be a bridge to a relationship with this young man. It worked.

Practicing English with Peter became my favorite morning half-hour during my year's work at the house. Most of my work was on my feet, running around. English lessons were a chance to sit down. But it was Peter himself who, on most days, made his lesson a highlight for me. He was eager to learn about American presidents. We went to the library, got him a card, and chose children's biographies of Abraham Lincoln, George Washington, and Franklin Roosevelt. Then, sitting side by side each day on the loveseat in the house's tiny library, we read them. He and I took turns reading them aloud for practice in both comprehension and pronunciation. Peter's patriotism extended from a curiosity about presidents to a keen interest in learning to sing "The Star-Spangled Banner." One day he asked me to help him write out the words in his spiral notebook. But to recite the words, I found myself having to sing the tune in places. When Peter had written all the words out, he wanted to sing it. I felt silly sitting on a loveseat beside an eager Asian man in the flagless library belting out "The Star-Spangled Banner." Our odd duet became one more occasion to bring out the zany in me!

At the end of each reading lesson, Peter took out his notebook to write what he called his "daily psalm." The subjects he chose for his compositions expressed his poetic nature: he wrote about the wind and the sky and the sun shining on the world. He often wrote phrases he'd learned singing in his family's church choir. Many days he wrote about his family. Sometimes, with a glint in his eye, he'd decide to write about my family. In pidgin English he asked me questions and expected me to recite the answers in good grammatical form so he could write them down. He wore a perpetual sly smile because my answers meant he knew me better. Occasionally he wanted to write something about his shame that he was a full grown man and yet had neither a wife nor the ability to take care of his parents. Adult males in his culture were expected to assume responsibility for their elderly parents, and he was keenly aware that he had not done this. I was reassured to see how readily he wrote and spelled English words. He needed help getting his sentences arranged grammatically and correctly, but his ideas emerged seemingly untainted by his mental illness. He told me in the course of our lessons, however, that he expected, according to pattern, to become mentally ill in the spring. I shared his anxiety as spring approached.

In the belief that work is a vital part of a mentally ill person's return to normal life, our vocational specialist helped those residents who asked for help and seemed to be ready to find jobs. At the house we had inaugurated a project in which we grew and sold lettuce and other greens from our greenhouse to Seattle restaurants. This meant our residents could have "in-house" work if they trained for it, planting the seeds and transplanting the tiny plants outside to our organic garden when they were ready. Peter participated in the training course for work in our greenhouse offered by two horticulturalists. Following the training, Peter was chosen as one of two clients who were given paid work in the greenhouse. He was slow but careful as he planted seeds. I took the training, and afterward, eager to learn the skills myself, volunteered to

Planting Seeds

Greenhouse light shines bright on your black hair.
From your palm your stubby fingers pluck one
small black seed after another to drop into
half-inch holes in soil-filled trays.

Beside yours, my finger moves to close the hole
so you will know where you have planted.
Two seeds drop into one hole.
"Two not good!" you falter.
"Two's okay." I assure.
I think but do not say:
Perfection is not possible.
The best is an enemy of the good.

You begin to hum. You like to plant.
This work may even lead to the payroll!
What follows does not matter.
Nothing matters. Everything matters.
Our fingers move in silence.

You begin to sing in a mellow baritone.
I join you in a faded alto.
"Jesus loves me, this I know."

I hope you do know.
I hope you sing now
not because "the Bible tells you so,"
but because now, planting escarole,
you sense your self to be part
of the whole singing,
seed-germinating universe.

supervise the seed planting. Peter's uncertainty about his own abilities made it a colossal task to boost his confidence each time he started some new activity. He had a host of physical complaints—"my stomach hurts," "my eyes not work today"—to excuse himself. But once he learned the routines of the greenhouse our sessions there were lively and enough fun that he wanted to go to them. One day, when we had had a particularly fun-filled time working together, I wrote my first poem, "Planting Seeds," about the greenhouse work.

Before long, Peter and I often had two work sessions together on any given day, one on the loveseat in the library, and one planting seeds in the greenhouse.

One thing that was important for Peter to do for his parents, who as recent Asian immigrants knew very little English, was help them with the official notices they received in the mail about matters such as their public housing. They shunted documents that confused them directly to Peter at the house, and he sought help from the English-speaking staff. The poem "Help!" on the following page suggests the process.

Peter's mother came often to see him, and she seemed eager while in the house to do little things for us in return. One night she expressed her gratitude by cooking for us. With house funds she purchased the ingredients for an Asian meal, and then she did the bulk of the cooking. The housemates were offered a delightful Asian meal that night, but Peter's pride was buried under his usual shyness as his housemates gobbled his mother's food. His mother spoke her pride in body language rather than words, and seemed equally pleased.

Like some other residents when they first came to the house, Peter was given a single room. He claimed he needed an introduction to group living without a roommate, and we agreed with him. We had six double rooms and only three single rooms. After about three months someone else came into the house who required a single room more than Peter did, and we asked him to move into a room with a roommate. He was hesitant, but we insisted. His roommate was a man named Simon who was not particularly happy with the roommate he had at the time. Peter knew Simon

Help!

You come to me waving an official paper:
a letter has passed through your parents'
sparse English to your uncertain tongue.

I telephone a bureau, explain the family's
lack of language. They claim your parents
must appear at a downtown office.
The danger: by a bureaucratic fluke
there's a threat to your family's housing.
I try an explanation. Your English makes
it gobbledygook. It is. I know
I'll not hear if your parents appear
but you'll run to me if they're evicted.

better than many of his other housemates, however, because they worked together happily in the greenhouse. Peter's move to Simon's room proved to be another significant step, not only in socializing both Simon and Peter, but in helping Peter become competent with English. The two became so fond of each other that much later, when Simon had been judged able to live independently and had moved out, Peter was unable to adjust to his new roommate, and it was decided that he should move out and share a house with Simon. Together both men took happily to independent living.

One winter day a cold took my voice, and at our lesson in the library, when I began to read aloud, Peter hushed my croaking. Instead, with his halting pronunciation, he read aloud from our book on Franklin Delano Roosevelt. We were both beginning to share a great regard for this president. The passage he read told of Roosevelt's dream of a United Nations and of how his sudden death threatened the realization of that dream. My mood that day was down, and quite suddenly there were tears of mourning running down my cheeks, right there in the lesson. To comfort me, Peter patted my knee.

Throughout the time I worked with Peter on language, he often returned to a theme best caught in the poem "If Not This, Still...That," on the following page.

Peter's physical complaints continued to provide reasons he could not work. Some days he claimed he couldn't see, or that there was an eyelash in his eye, or that he'd had a dizzy spell. Since I could never be sure if his complaints were serious enough to genuinely handicap him, I tended to ignore them and suggest we work despite them. He usually went along when I insisted. One day, when he had initially said he was too tired to work, a housemate came to the door of the library in the middle of our lesson, complained that he ached all over, and asked Peter to give him a massage. Shelving his own ailments, Peter got up and we interrupted our lesson so that he and the other man could retreat to the living room. There his housemate lay on the floor while Peter offered his version of a massage. It was a rare resident who was able to get out of himself enough to enjoy doing something for someone else.

I encouraged Peter to listen to the news to improve his English.

If Not This, Still...That

"No work today," you grunt.
But you still want to sit with me.
"So...go get your book."
We sit enfolded by a loveseat.
You read about Abraham Lincoln.
"The print—too small." We stop.
Still, you're willing to write.
I help you phrase your litany.
You print in your plain style,
bemoan your father's painful feet and
your parents' "sacrifices" for you—
you know this word from church.
You're ashamed you cannot care for them.
They're too old to care for you.

I explain to you about my children.
"I'll go on making what you call 'sacrifices'
gladly for them till I'm old, just because
they're my children. Love's
not a product, it produces."
My words fall into the dark cave of your mind.
Your English fails on verbs like produce.
Your culture commands you to care for parents.

Now Lincoln park enfolds you, me, and three
housemates. The wind gusts around
a frigid sun, but you sing beside us.
Driving home you ask to stop
at the Texaco store, go in and buy
us all drinks. For me you choose
spring water, since you know my tastes,
and would care for me.

Once, when I found him in the living room watching the news on television, I dropped into an easychair beside him. We were hearing about the president's peccadilloes when Peter's housemate Hugo walked into the room. As Hugo sometimes did, he patted me on the head lightly and affectionately.

Peter saw this gesture, jumped up, raised both fists, and took a boxer's stance. "You don't do!" he growled. Hugo, unaccustomed to anyone thwarting his spontaneity, raised his tattooed arms in a lackadaisical response and clenched his fists less in defense than in imitation. "I respect you," he pleaded, looking at me, his eyes red, his bare feet dancing (he had traded his shoes for cigarettes). Hugo's inept fists continued to thrash in the air. Peter went on threatening him with fists up. "I respect you," Hugo said again to me.

Some time before this incident I heard Hugo express his false belief that Peter was Vietnamese. Because of the war he didn't like the Vietnamese. Did Peter sense Hugo's hostility? Were his fists up for more than Hugo's mere pat on my head?

No time to decide. "It's all right, Peter. Hugo respects me," I stammered, and both men sat down.

In May Peter's mental illness began to engulf him in a changed way. The staff at the house, including me, became more alert to and saddened by the deteriorated mental state we observed in him. The poem "The Pendulum Has Swung Too Far" describes my reaction. Our medical team kept alert and treated Peter with closer monitoring of his medications for about two months until slowly he became more effective again in all the activities at the house.

As Peter was recovering, our vocational counselor had a job open. Our clients had a good record with a restaurant owner who had only a few employees. The relaxed atmosphere he maintained in the work he offered our clients meant they were able to adjust well to his requirements. Our vocational counselor didn't want to lose the opportunity of this job, and Peter seemed the most likely candidate for it. Peter, however, was hesitant. He said he'd had jobs in the outside world before and he'd been slow, unable to keep up a pace that satisfied his employer. On the other hand, we were sure from the thorough way he worked in the house that he could handle this job. His mental state had become more and more dependable after his trouble during the spring. We persuaded him to "just

The Pendulum Has Swung Too Far

You leap to life awry.
Your speech bleeds words that
don't make sense.

The pain behind your bloodshot eyes
lashes out in stumbles when nothing trips you.
I tell myself bipolar means
this too will pass.

Vive la Compagnie

You've come through the manic phase.
Now a new shoot rises
from the core of you.
In the greenhouse,
you move dirt with dispatch,
plant seeds with aplomb,
listen with grasp and sing:

"Let ev'ry good fellow
now join in the song."
Yes viva. Viva to meds,
viva to watchfulness,
viva to life begun again.

try" this job. He worked two mornings a week, pleasing the employer and pleasing himself. When the job came to an end, he took another job in a larger restaurant, washing dishes and doing simple food preparation. That employer liked him well enough to hope to teach him more responsible cooking jobs.

Someone convinced Peter that he needed more exercise, and he went swimming with us once. Was his innate dignity somehow injured by that jaunty swimming party? It was difficult to know. He appeared to have a good time, but he avoided subsequent trips to the pool. I continued to invite him and hope. Often the reason he gave for his refusal to join in this activity was that he had to go to some administrative office on either his family's or his own business. He knew this excuse would impress me, since I knew how much he wanted to help his parents. Now, unlike them, he knew enough English. He could deal with the American bureaucracy!

Later, when I observed how completely Peter coped in his day-to-day life, held down a job where they thought highly of his work, and had returned again to singing in his church choir, I thought of the words of an old hymn: "When friends by shame are undefiled, how can I keep from singing?" The poem "Vive la Compagnie" suggests the spirit of our singing.

SIMON

WHEN I THINK of Peter, my mind often leaps to his housemate Simon. Both young men were what I might call "clean livers." Simon ate a healthy diet, refrained from smoking and drinking, and lived a healthy life-style even before the onset of his mental illness. Simon attributed the way he lived to his religious faith, which he took so seriously that, rather than deviate from its rules, he shunned celebrating Christmas and birthdays.

Simon had considerable work experience before his mental breakdown occurred. He became mentally ill when the going got rough at the bank where he was working. He was a handsome young man whose thoroughly respectable looks qualified him for work in a bank. But although he possessed superior intelligence, his mental instability somehow meant he had difficulty withstanding the pressure of work in a bank.

When he'd lived in the house long enough to convince us of his abilities, he told our vocational counselor he would like to work with flowers and she obtained a job for him in a florist's shop. He lasted only a week and a half. According to rumor, when he resigned he told his employer that she had made a mistake by hiring a mentally ill person, since such people were not dependable. Many of his housemates were dependable in their jobs. Perhaps Simon's strong religious faith, coupled with his mental illness, made him feel like an outsider. In any case, this particular new job—with flowers, of all things—somehow threatened him. The poem on the next page chronicles one of Simon's moods.

We at the house knew Simon was capable of being dependable at work because he was so responsible in our greenhouse. He was the person we could count on to walk from the house where he lived, a long block away from the main house, to keep the tiny seedlings in the greenhouse watered. When there were special greenhouse jobs that did not involve heavy work—he didn't volunteer for the heavier garden work—he was always willing to do them. It appeared that he sometimes did extra jobs in the greenhouse more because he wanted to please us than because he wanted the work. He thrived on demonstrating this kind of dependability on the job, and the house's "Growing Solutions" program—we grew and sold organic greens to restaurants—very much needed his dependability.

Simon and Peter became "a pair" after living together a year in the main house and almost as long in one of our nearby supported-living houses. When Simon was first in the main house, he was bothered by and discontent with the first roommate he drew. There came a time when we had to make a shift in the house, and we decided that despite Peter's claim that he could not endure living with a roommate, we would move him from his single room to share a room with Simon. Once Peter had learned that he could live with someone, he also spoke and understood English better. Simon also learned that he enjoyed life more with a good friend steadily present. Because I knew that Simon might want to honor his friend, when I made a special cake for Peter's birthday I asked Simon if he wanted to help. I wished I hadn't asked. Simon's loyalty to his religious faith meant that he could not in good conscience do anything to acknowledge a celebration of Peter's

The Healing Place

Grumpy this morning you
complain you're hungry
and our food looks like grunge.
You make but one commitment:
to plant seeds in the greenhouse.
Go out early. You come exactly
when you say you will.
Greenhouse magic—
dibbling dirt, fooling
with your Korean buddy—
signals a new mood.
You who are Chinese,
Norwegian, Irish, French, and Blackfoot Indian
ask: "What do you get when you cross a
psychic with a comedian?
A happy medium!
How do you like my joke?
I made it up."
You grin as pride
buries your grumps.

birthday. “I’ll give you a present any other day,” he told Peter, and proceeded to show me his regret at refusing to participate by being more spirited than usual in the other ways he entered into the house’s activities. He overcame his usual reluctance to play bingo and joined in. He talked about his part in a Shakespeare play in high school, and how engrossing and exhausting it had been. He made up jokes. In short, that day he was livelier than he was when he was his normal, quiet self. That day I sensed that, either consciously or unconsciously, he was showing me that while he might not celebrate birthdays, he approved of the celebrating world more than I might have thought.

To these two young men the house could be said to have offered more than it usually offered to its residents. It gave each of them a long-term friend, someone who understood his mental handicap. Each of these two young men not only made allowances for his housemate’s illness, but at the same time appeared grateful for the sheltering nature of such a friendship. Each of them had yearned for a mate, but that had not yet been their destiny. This connection, this loyalty they had found, was perhaps the next best thing.

CAROL

Whooptedoo! Someone with Skill in Her Hands

I heard Carol before I ever saw her. I hadn't been aware that a new resident was coming. Peter and I were working on his English upstairs in the library one warm day when a cadence of cackling laughter floated through the open window from the covered patio below. Ah, a rare lighthearted woman! We hadn't had an upbeat woman in the house since I'd been there. Let such ebullience spread! Whose was this laugh?

When our lesson was finished I padded downstairs and glanced out onto the terrace. Sitting beside one of the virile-looking men of the house, looking glum, was a young woman whose blond curly hair made her appear younger than her sallow skin suggested. I guessed the laughter had been hers, but now her drooping look belied the glee I had heard. She needed a welcome.

"You must have just come. I'm Judy, a volunteer here."

"I'm Carol. I remember you from when I visited before."

Chagrined that I recalled her only vaguely, I glanced downward and noticed she was wearing a cast on her leg. "What did you do to your leg?"

"I broke my ankle at the hospital. Its okay now. They took the cast off, but now I wear the cast just to protect it."

If her cast had been removed, what had made her decide to put it back on again? It wasn't the time to ask. "Where did they suggest you settle in?" She indicated the single room we often bestow on new residents, then turned to the man she'd been laughing with.

"I fooled them. They wanted to keep me at the state hospital." She held a piece of gray pottery aloft and laughed again. "See what I made in the pottery studio?" The mug in her hand looked like it had been made by a real craftsman. She was justly proud of it.

Carol's arrival gave me a sense of anticipation. Most of our residents were not interested in making things with their hands. Here was a new person whom I might be able to interest in crafts. Indeed, here was a person who seemed capable of a kind of refreshing normality. I decided not to read her history, but to take her for just what I found her to be, encourage her in activities that would give her a sense of her own capability, and watch her begin to cope. In those early days I had not yet observed how Carol's delusions held her captive to her self-doubts. I wrote the poem opposite when I became more aware of her delusions.

Several mornings after she arrived at the house, when I entered the living room I found Carol sitting dejected, her chin drooping on her chest. "How are you, friend?" I asked.

"They want me to change my body, but I like it like it is."

"Who wants you to change? We like your body just fine!"

"But they want me to go for a physical."

"That's so we can keep your body healthy, not change it." Her distrust of a physical examination seemed too deeply embedded to try to argue her out of it. My best course was to distract her. "You were telling me yesterday how you cooked Brussels sprouts? What did you tell me?"

"You put them on a tray, sprinkle them with salt and pepper, put butter on them, and cook them lightly in the oven." She seemed to want to be distracted.

"Sounds good. Will you help me do that this afternoon?"

"My body's not so all the men in the house can use me. They don't like it that I don't wear a bra. That's just the way I am. They want me to change my body."

"All of us need physicals in order to stay healthy," I assured.

The day wore on. In the afternoon Carol chose to go out walking with us and slogged energetically along the path by Puget Sound despite her cast. She made the Brussels sprouts when it was time, and when I had put on my coat to leave and was already out the door, I heard her call, "Judith. . . ." Her need sounded urgent, but my bus was due across the street. "Judith. . . ." I hadn't time to wait. But I glanced back, saw her nearly running on her cast-clad leg, and stopped. When she reached me she cupped her hands about my ear and whispered into it, "You are the light of my world."

What About Bad Genes?

Creative minds have been known to survive
any kind of bad training....
—Anna Freud

Your mind jumps
from zany madness
to a crazy gladness
where your laugh crackles,
your delusion fades,
and you allow you
and me to be fey.

You have a flair
for cooking Brussels sprouts.
This house is brighter
since you've been here.
On the days when your
delusions pop like popcorn
I'm deflated, since on your
better days you rise above reality
and I float high with you.

"Thank you. It's lovely to be told that," I said as I saw my bus and dashed across the street, flagging it as I ran.

I climbed onto the bus, sank onto a seat, and mused that tomorrow Carol's light might well go out again.

Even though I had not read Carol's case history, I still knew she had grown up in a large family on a farm, because she often spoke fondly of her early life there. She told stories of milking cows and feeding animals. I also got the sense that she felt her mother had abandoned her, whether that was actually the case or not. At Christmas, when Carol's sister sent her a hat she had knitted for her, it became more than a prized possession. She wore it inside the house and out, and told many people her sister had made it for her. That hand-knit hat was more than itself. It was a sign there was someone in the cold world outside who cared for her enough to knit something for her.

Hugo was a resident whose fantasy life centered around sex. Carol, ripe for a crush on some man, adopted Hugo. They began to pair up on outings and made time for each other in the house as well. One morning Carol asked me to come to her room. "I have something I want to show you. I'll read it to you." It was a poem in four stanzas she had written to Hugo. "I will love you forever," she had written. Then, with flowery language and impeccable penmanship, she had expanded the idea. When she'd finished reading aloud, I moved cautiously from what was sublime for Carol to what was mundane for me. I suggested that she and Hugo might like to come with me to help do the grocery shopping. Food buying was one of the tasks the staff did for the house only when there were residents willing to go along to help. Carol would be doing me a favor by going, and I knew she relished being helpful. She agreed to go, and therefore, it was a given that Hugo would go. I offered her a ninety-cent coupon I'd been given for a large bottle of Coca-Cola. As we drove to Safeway in the van, I noticed she gave a dollar and the coupon to Hugo. Hugo, who adored Coke—or anything with caffeine in it—marched straight into the store's beverage aisle, selected a bottle of Coke, planted it in the grocery cart, and went outside again for a smoke. Carol, by contrast, stuck with me to help find the items on our grocery list and load the cart. Before we finished, however, she too grew weary and retreated outside for a smoke. I continued filling the cart and was nearly finished when Carol, clearly out of sorts, rejoined me. "He needs to grow up," she muttered as she removed the bottle of Coke from the grocery cart and went off to return it to the shelf.

A few moments later Hugo shuffled in, reported to where I was wheeling the cart, and volunteered to find some of the groceries. "I'm tired of being treated like a child," he growled.

Fifteen minutes later we all climbed into the van again, and things seemed normal between Carol and Hugo. I wondered, however, about the difference between Carol's love as she expressed it on paper and as it played out in reality. How did she deal with this contrast when she was actually with Hugo? Lovers have a habit of idealizing their loves. Did her dull days become brighter in the glow of being in love with love? This twosome suffered what looked to me like a vast divide between dreams and reality. Hugo was perpetually unwashed, inept at most things, and unable to concentrate. Carol was clearly capable of many things, but lived captive to her delusions. Still every human needs affection, and I guessed that Carol had somehow learned to use her imagination to rise above the reality that was Hugo. The house had brought them together, given them a setting in which to express their needs to both give affection and gain affection, even if their relationship wobbled. That setting was a gift the house could offer them. The house had been the setting for other liaisons, and would continue to be. This particular one, for all its off and on again quality, meant these two people were basically happier in their "handicapped" existence.

Carol's favorite activities turned out to be those in which she could make cookies or fashion something else that helped her feel like Lady Bountiful bestowing the fruits of her efforts on her housemates. Like many another person, she needed to be needed. She admired the quality of usefulness, both in her fellow humans and also in animals. She often spoke of the cows on her family's farm. Her fondness for them seemed due in part to the fact that they so bountifully bestowed milk on her family. Carol, too, was never happier than when she felt herself to be giving. One day, when we had made brownies, she liked them, but she liked even more taking them from the kitchen out to the greenhouse and passing them out to her housemates working there.

When Carol went on the library outings she was drawn to the

music tapes rather than the books. Checking tapes out one at a time, she watched the due dates on them carefully to make sure she got them back on time. At night music floated from the tape player in her room. Once she thought she had lost a tape and was so troubled she wouldn't go to the library until I went with her to look for it in her room. When we found it under the bed, her immense relief seemed out of proportion to the loss. I had to learn, however, that our residents could attach meaning beyond my understanding to losses. I was only glad Carol was released to go to the library again and select other tapes.

Carol had a nimble mind, one that created countless ideas of things to do and replays of her childhood before the onset of her mental illness. In my time with her I tried to ignore the delusional part of her thinking and concentrate on her love of fun. She had a fey streak that made her a delightful person to do things with. Once, when I took a group to the aquarium, she hooked up with Hugo and they moved from tank to tank quickly and exuberantly. Her delight in watching the meandering, colorful fish and her fascination with the sea otters at play made the visit come alive.

Partly because I liked Carol so much, I decided to follow through on an idea I'd had to stage a picnic for all our residents at my home on an island beach. The agency's executive director, who lived on the same island, was enthusiastic about the idea and offered his help. The program supervisor was also eager to help and made a colorful flyer announcing the event. We invited all the past and present residents I knew. We planned it for June, when we hoped the weather would allow us to be outside. We'd have a beach fire so we could roast hot dogs on sticks and sit about on driftwood logs while we ate. Nineteen people, including several from the surrounding supported-living houses, climbed into the van and filed onto the ferry. I described the picnic spot to Carol at length and told her I hoped she'd help serve the crowd. I figured she'd enjoy being kind of co-hostess. We spoke of the plans as if there were no doubt she would come. However, because my home is a two-hour commute from the agency's house, I didn't go to the house on the day of the picnic. Instead I relied on the staff to organize the transportation and accompany the people who chose to come. The guests arrived. Everyone in the house at that time piled out of the cars except Carol, Hugo, and Myrtle. When Carol wasn't there my disappointment told me that there was a sense in which I had planned the outing for her. I had somehow wanted to hear Carol's loud laughter ringing out on our beach.

The picnic provided a string of memorable moments. Before we ate, the executive director drew lines in the sand and organized us into two teams for a roaring game of capture-the-flag. Sand flew, rules were bent, people scuffled. Players worked up big appetites. We each had to roast our own hot dog on a stick. The roasting operation took more patience than some of our picnickers were willing to give it, and there was bargaining among the crew to get a friend to roast an extra one. Only a few wieners dropped into the fire from burnt-through sticks. When we were finished eating, people stood around uncertain what to do with themselves. They were not adept at talking with each other.

I returned to the house the next day vowing to schedule another picnic next season. In the meantime I would find some inducement that would elicit Carol's promise to actually come. At the same time I planned my own response: to be pleased if she came, and to refuse to feel let down if she didn't. I had learned that a large dose of ambivalence and uncertainty go with the diagnosis of schizophrenia. I had experienced Carol's ambivalence and how it played into her fears. I knew she didn't respond well to being pressured, and I couldn't expect to overcome her fears every time they made her shilly-shally. When the second annual picnic rolled around, I told her I needed her help to serve the food. The morning of the picnic she went so far as to get into one of the cars. After a brief moment, however, she panicked. "Tell Judy I'm sorry, I couldn't make it," she said, and got out again.

Some months later Carol's physical examination revealed she had breast cancer. That knowledge first elicited denial from her, and later gave a field day to her fears. She clung to misinformation about the surgery that might be required, and Hugo didn't help. He stood behind Carol, holding her as if to protect her, and told me, "They're going to take my woman's titty."

The added attention Carol had from her family helped to calm her fears and make her ready for the surgery. She was high and bubbly the day after when she came back to the house loaded with all the gifts she'd been given—a fancy nightgown, flowers, a balloon. Her high faded and her fears grew, however, when she developed an infection that took special treatment. When the report came saying that the surgery had got all the cancerous tissue and that it hadn't had time to spread, the house rejoiced with Carol. At the same time we continued to monitor her health closely. The important thing for Carol was to be able to get back to a place where she could feel herself needed and giving. It's a limping nag of a life, but she's riding it.

HUGO

Raptor Eyes

THE RUMORS about Hugo made him seem scary. His out-of-state family was sending him to our house in the hope we would keep him out of prison and help him learn to behave. He had had problems in almost every other mental institution he'd been in. He'd been in prison for a number of years, and he was rumored to be a kind of sexual predator. I was still new as a volunteer in the house. The rumors made me wary.

One stormy morning I came to the house and found Hugo in the dining room as a new resident. What did his hungry eyes following me mean? They struck me as raptor eyes. Was it he who had made the mess in the dining room? The table where we make the coffee was littered with Equal, powdered cream wrappers, and the powder itself. Hugo was dishevelled and jumpy that first day as well. He spoke angrily to the social work student assigned to complete the "advance directives" the house needed to have on file for him. "No, don't suck me. Don't revive me if I'm breathless." The uncertain student taking his wrath was bewildered. What had so irritated him? Did he really mean he didn't want CPR or mouth-to-mouth resuscitation if he were found on the verge of death? Didn't he want to be revived? I learned later that, indeed, he was angry at something else: he'd missed his cigarette draw that morning. He'd let loose in that tirade most probably because he'd been deprived of his nicotine fix.

The next morning, when I walked into the dining room, he was standing beside the coffee machine watching it drip coffee down onto its burner. "Where's the coffee pot?" I asked. "Can we find it, put it in place to catch the coffee we're making?"

"You look so good, it's better than diddlin' with myself," he said.

I slammed the coffee pot under the stream of coffee and speculated. He'd no doubt had his tobacco fix that day.

Later that morning I towelled up the coffee he had spilt on the floor. He saw me and something—was it guilt?—made him ask to kiss me. "Just on the cheek?" he pleaded.

"Okay," I relented, and he pecked.

On those first days he was in the house he wanted hugs almost every time he found himself at close quarters in the kitchen with me. The poem on the following page suggests the context in which he wanted hugs as a reward.

For me, to forbid someone to give me a mere peck on the cheek was an odd experience. I wanted to respond to Hugo's clear need to express his affection innocently in hugs. My intuition told me that he needed to be around a woman whom he didn't threaten, who wasn't afraid of him. My age meant I could be that woman for him, but at the same time I knew that Hugo was the sort of person for whom I had to set boundaries—limits of behavior beyond which he would not be allowed to go. I began to accept his hugs when they came at logical times, refuse them in a friendly way when he wanted them at inappropriate times.

I had the same ambivalence about Hugo's perpetually food-stained shirt. When we were headed out of the house and he had a dirty shirt on, I asked him to change. If he was only going to be in the house I avoided having to correct him constantly, when most of the time he looked like a shabby, red-eyed terror anyway. He was completely heedless of his own sloppiness, and the corollary of his heedlessness was that he had no idea of his effect on other people.

Early on Hugo learned he could offer help in exchange for a hug when I was in the kitchen and the dishes were undone. Later, learning that other residents traded extra chores for pop, he changed and asked to earn a Coke. Since caffeine seemed to overstimulate our residents, we didn't offer them caffeinated coffee. At canteen time, however, we let them buy Coca-Cola knowing it was full of caffeine and might shoot them sky high. With caffeine, as with so many other things, it proved difficult to be consistent. Indeed, very soon it struck me that with Hugo, as with my own children, it was important to save my "nos" and "dont's" for times

Work for Hugs

Today the chart for breakfast dishes has
no name. I plead to Myrtle. "Will you do them?"
(She loves water. Beneath a stream from
the faucet she swishes dishes with dash.)
Myrtle says, "No," but you cry,
"I'll do them," and I decide to show
you how to draw water, add soap,
load the dishwasher, albeit awry.

You accept my teaching, talk motor
chitchat (with your inner voices),
finish, go upstairs, don a rare clean shirt,
come down, hang out, slop
the floor with spills of decaf,
bug your pals for cigarettes.

The lunch chart has another blank for dishes.
"I'll do it for a hug," you say. (My hero!)
"I'll pay you when you're done," I promise.
"Marry me! I want a Mrs. Gramma."
"No. I'd only be your damn ma."
"Then in heaven be my Gramma!"
"Does heaven have a Grammahood?"

when they really mattered. When I hoarded them, he responded readily to my verbal restraints.

Occasionally Hugo did something that made me want to hug him quite as much as he wanted to hug me. Even when he wore a coffee-stained shirt and frayed pants that drooped beneath his heels, his round beaming face made him seem innocent, lovable. Sometimes.

At first Hugo seemed hesitant about leaving the house to join us on outings. Early on he traded his boots for cigarettes, went about the house barefoot, and so didn't have footwear for going out. However, he slowly learned that there were adventures to be had—picnics at the zoo, exciting things to be seen, trips to the aquarium, laser shows at the science center—if he risked going with the group on outings. He began to make sure he signed up for enough chores each week to earn the privilege of going on outings. He also began to let himself be prompted to wear shoes, although his shoestrings usually flopped about his ankles.

When he appeared to need fewer hugs, I figured he had found an outlet for his libido in the house. Early on he had told me "On the third day in the house, I had sex with that old one." I sensed, however, he was telling me that he wouldn't be having sex again because it had not been altogether satisfactory. But Carol had recently read me a love poem she had written Hugo. I guessed that no one had ever tried to teach him appropriate ways to express his approval of a woman. Could I? I hesitated. He had little control of his impulses. Was he capable of learning control if I had no other training method than suggestions? I knew he was easily hurt by strong suggestions, so I began to suggest things to him gently. At the same time I observed his housemates becoming used to the outlandish things he did and accepting him with less annoyance. When his craziness began to draw less attention, he behaved in less intrusive ways.

It became a challenge, then, to get Hugo to do something active and constructive. Most of the time he lay about the house sleeping and gaining weight. Since he'd mentioned once that he would like to learn to play the guitar, I borrowed a guitar from a friend. "The deal is this: my friend will give it to you if you learn to play it," I told him. "She'll take it back if you don't learn." Then I asked my son Craig, a passable guitar player and a patient teacher, to come to the house and give lessons to Hugo. We staged the lessons in the living room at a time when others who might be interested could be there. I hoped, naïvely, that an enthusiasm for guitar playing might catch on.

Craig came one afternoon, tuned our borrowed guitar, and pronounced its tone good. He had brought a book that gave simple guitar chords for a number of well-known songs. Hugo had no interest in anything so constricting as a book. Instead, another young man, Alan, took the book and studied the chords. Hugo could not be persuaded to sit down with the guitar beside Craig to work at any chords. Instead he danced about Craig, clearly fascinated with this guitar teacher as a person. "How could anyone so big have come out of you?" Hugo asked me.

Craig worked with Alan for a while before he went off, leaving the music book in case Hugo wanted to work on his own. While Craig was there Hugo had flitted about steadily, unable to concentrate, but I was hardly surprised. Somehow he was embarrassed. He couldn't bring himself to sit, appear to work, and be inept under the eye of a stranger.

Several days later Hugo asked for the guitar. He sat down with it, strummed it rapidly and randomly, as if he knew exactly what he was doing, and pretended to be Elvis, who he claimed "I really like." His enthusiasm lasted perhaps five minutes before his concentration lagged and he put the guitar back in its case.

One other day, when the weather was warm, Hugo darted about, asked for the guitar, and insisted I sit beside him while he strummed it. He set the stage with two plastic chairs outside the house in the cement driveway, led me to one of them, and mimicked singing me love songs. Smack in the middle of the driveway we sat together on those two dirty white chairs while he strummed vigorously. The mock romance was complete when he made noises as if he were singing to me. I mustered an outward calm, but inwardly I admitted I was flattered.

A new side of Hugo began to come out. If he liked someone, he not only wanted to be with him or her, but also needed to give that person some tangible sign of his affection. Often, when we walked on Seattle's Alki Beach promenade, he moseyed up beside me and offered me a swig from his bottle of Coke. He began to shuffle across the street to the bus stop with me when I left for the day.

One day while we waited he pulled from the pocket of his coffee-spotted raincoat a packet of gummy bears and insisted on pouring a handful out into my palm. Ignoring my protests that he was giving me more than I wanted, he followed that bounty with a small unopened packet of Fritos he had been given that day on the zoo outing. "Take it, take it, I don't want it."

For all this bounty he needed money, and he urged us to give him a job in the house's garden project. The staff garden supervisor tried him several times, hovering about him with ready suggestions as to what he should do and how he should do it, but Hugo couldn't sustain a thread of concentration. He would work with gusto for perhaps five minutes, then stop and stand watching others. He might work again when prompted, and several minutes later wander off.

Hugo's approach to swimming with the group was ambivalent, and the first time he went with us to swim, I was hesitant about taking him. I wasn't sure he could swim. Would he need a kind of supervision I wouldn't be able to give him? He emerged from the dressing room at the outdoor saltwater pool wearing the bathing suit I had collected from a friend's discard drawer, and surveyed the pool's crowd. Then, before I could speak to him, he dove straight into the deep end.

His next move was to swim to me in a passable crawl stroke and offer to protect me. He wanted to make sure I was safe, since he wasn't certain I could swim. After that initial swimming outing he joined us often on our weekly jaunts to an indoor pool. But he was unpredictable. Sometimes he spent the whole time with us in the water. Other times he climbed up the ladder and returned to the locker room after only getting wet. Once, when he hadn't put on his bathing suit and paced beside the pool wearing a grungy, food-stained raincoat, the lifeguard requested that we bring to the pool "only those who will actually swim." If we had enthusiastic swimmers in the pool, we could usually get a game of tag going, and Hugo entered those games with enthusiasm. I kidded him once about this eagerness to play tag. "You like it 'cause it's one of the few times you can chase girls legitimately." He heard me, but didn't protest.

Once, however, he tagged a young woman by swimming up behind her and kissing the wet black hair on the back of her head.

"I don't like that," she objected.

"You mustn't do that," I said, and Hugo was hurt. So hurt he left the pool and dressed to go. The poem "Swimming," on the next page, suggests what happened on one occasion at the pool.

One morning Hugo confronted me as I came in the door. "Hey, it's my birthday!"

"Then let's bake a cake!" As I spoke I glanced at a young woman who I knew liked to bake cakes with me. She remained stony faced. I knew she'd been "on" with Hugo during the previous week when he had money, but now she either hadn't heard my suggestion or wasn't keen on doing anything to honor Hugo. Since I didn't know what had been going on between them, I said no more.

If there was to be no cake, we arranged to celebrate when we all went on the swimming outing. When we arrived at the pool, however, Hugo put on his bathing suit, got into the pool, and paddled about only long enough to get wet. Then suddenly he lifted his chin, peered out of the pool as if he were looking for something, and pushed his belly up and over the pool's edge. Then, having caught a glimpse of the Coke machine in the foyer, he shot up the ladder and out.

We got home in time for money draw at two o'clock, and Hugo learned he could draw the three dollars left in his monthly account. "I wanna go to the Luna for a milkshake," he told the staff person dispensing the funds. Suspicious of Hugo's spending habits, she asked me to go with him to make sure he actually spent his money on a milkshake. "Let's go," I said. "We'll get a milk shake and ask them for two straws."

Walking the block to the Luna Park Café, Hugo wavered. "Maybe I'll get coffee."

"Ice cream's better for you." I figured he was hoping for a caffeine fix, and I knew I wanted a milkshake. On arriving at the café, Hugo pulled three wadded bills from his pocket and thrust all but one at the waitress.

"It's my birthday. We want milkshakes," he said.

"Can we share one?" I asked the waitress, since I was fairly sure the two dollars he'd offered wouldn't stretch to two milkshakes.

The waitress brought two tall glasses, one topped with whipped

Swimming

Today you make no excuses,
don't leave the pool after two kicks and a yell.
You grab a noodle, bob about chatting
your usual jagged chatter. This
about a hunt in Texas woods.
At length you insist I float, balance
my body on your outstretched hands,
You want me to kick, lie on the water.
I comply.
You linger longer, show your strokes
stronger until you climb the ladder, dress,
float home and boast to another counselor:
"I held Gramma up in the water!"

cream and a candle burning beside a red cherry. Whooptedoo! I wasn't sure I wanted to project the picture of two lovers drinking from two straws out of one glass.

While I sipped my milkshake, Hugo chattered. "I spent thirty years in prison, you know." (The last time he'd talked about his prison term it had been eighteen years.)

"Since you were in prison, why isn't your language foul?"

"I know better than to speak that way in front of ladies," he answered. Then, "What does your husband think when we go off like this?"

I had no time to answer because at that moment a waitress passed and he flagged her. "Hey, will you bring me a cup of coffee?" he asked, waving the dollar bill he'd crumpled in his hand.

Then he noticed two young women speaking to each other intently in a booth across the way and yelled at them. "Hey!"

They ignored him. He called "Hey" once more before he gave up and focused his attention on me again.

He got up to leave when his shake was half-finished, and the waitress had not brought the coffee. Instead, at the cash register he proffered his dollar bill for a takeout coffee. Dribbles of coffee spilled on the sidewalk as he toted it back to the house.

"What'll your husband think?" he asked again. He asked this at least once every time we did anything together.

"He knows I love him. He isn't bothered when I have other friends," I assured him. But if Hugo heard my assurances, he seemed unable to absorb the idea that a chat, a mere activity in tandem, would not be seen as threatening to my husband.

That first week that I encountered Hugo in the house his eyes looked to me like "raptor eyes." Later, when I looked at his eyes their rims were red, but the eyes themselves had a softness about them that I could never have associated with anything so predatory as a raptor. Nor did the shaved head and curly ponytail he had persuaded someone to give him fit my image of him. When he lashed out about "them bad Vietnamese" or "damned coloreds," I sensed his strong opinions were more habitual prejudice than genuine hatred. Hugo's bids for affection seemed so urgent, so innocent, that it was hard to think of him hating anyone. Hugo's difficulty in getting along seemed to have to do with his inability to understand what were appropriate gestures toward his friends. He acted on every impulse that came to him. This meant he spontaneously accosted strangers, sometimes annoying them, sometimes amusing them. Self-discipline was a commodity he was unable to grasp.

Several months after we celebrated Hugo's birthday, the folks at the Luna Park asked that he not come to their café any more. He could not be tamed. He would not refrain from greeting the other customers too forcefully.

The Luna Park Café might have rejected him, but that didn't matter much to Hugo because it was outside the house. Hugo seemed quite content to be living at the house now that he had lived there long enough to feel that his housemates tolerated him. There was even Carol, who seemed genuinely to want his erratic affection. Because he needed to both get and give affection, the house was a place where he seemed content to settle in, feeling accepted and cared about. I guessed the acceptance he felt in that living situation made for one of the rare times he had lived anywhere contentedly in over forty years of life.

DAPHNE

A Need to Give

YES, SHE WAS A person of color, a colorful personality. A woman who came to us having graduated down from her own apartment. A woman who cherished and protected her dignity. A woman whose anger, when it bloomed, was so blustery as to make her seem adolescent. Daphne had a diagnosed mental illness, but to most outward appearances she seemed eccentric rather than mentally ill. To us she denied her illness, and in her human relationships she very nearly pulled that denial off.

Hearsay went that her family had insisted she come to a more supervised living situation because, living and cooking alone in her own apartment, she had nearly caused a serious fire. Her other folly, rumor had it, was to run up huge credit card bills buying things like diamond-studded cufflinks for her boyfriend. There was no controlling her, and her family decided she required a closer watch than they could provide to keep her in check. Perhaps we were doomed from the start when she came to us, since money was her issue and we were to become her "protective payee." This meant that her Social Security (SSI) funds would come to us from the state and we would have to rob her of her sense of autonomy by first deducting her room and board and then doling out the remainder of her money to her in small increments each week.

Daphne's friends were important to her. Thank God I turned out to be one of them. When I plunked myself down in the living room with my knitting, hoping a resident would express interest in learning to knit, Daphne saw my yarn and wanted some. Not because she wanted to learn to knit, but because she already knew how to crochet. Two of the other younger residents had tried to learn to knit and failed. When she saw me knitting, Daphne wheeled around, marched upstairs, returned with a wad of bright purple wool, and thrust it in my hand. It turned out to be a pair of misshapen baby booties, for a tiny infant. For Daphne the most important thing about them was that I was her friend and she was proud to give them to me. The poem on the facing page describes why she crocheted.

From the day she gave me the booties until she left I made a point of finding enough yarn to keep Daphne busy crocheting. Once a yarn shop owner gave me a hoard of leftover yarns. I brought them to Daphne and fed on her delight. She particularly liked having so many balls of baby-pale yellow, and crocheted some six or seven pairs of booties. It meant she could go to the baby shower of a friend armed with two pairs of yellow booties for the young mother. Then she took the remaining pairs down the street to the Luna Park Café. When she had circulated to each of the booths on one side of the café, urging customers to purchase her baby booties, the café management quietly but firmly asked her to leave. Money was her issue. She needed money in order to renew her image of herself as a bountiful giver.

Money was merely the primary issue over which Daphne quarreled with the house administration. She also had other issues. To be dignified required that she be clean, and dignity was a pillar of her view of herself. Not only did she have to be clean, the *house* had to be clean as well in order to reinforce her sense of living right. When she did the dishes, which wasn't often, she usually hurried through too fast to leave the kitchen genuinely clean. But clean bathrooms were a must. She refused to take a shower when the condition of the shower stall did not meet her high standards. Sporadically, she went to Tom's cleaning closet, got some staff person to open it for her, and gathered the equipment to give the shower a scrub.

Her acute need for money meant that Daphne filled out numerous job applications without waiting for our vocational counselor to offer her help. When she appeared at any business, such as the storage facility next door, however, it was important to her that she had attractive and appropriate clothing to wear. "I can't go there. I don't have anything to wear," she said once.

"What about that red blouse you wore yesterday?"

To Crochet Is to Give Away

When I come in the morning
you tell me you've prayed for me.
When I bring you yarn to crochet,
you fashion a tangle-riddled pair of booties
for my granddaughter's doll.

When you call me your "play mom,"
I'm intrigued to be maternally
connected to the cream-black sturdy
spine I washed the day you asked me to
scrub your back in the shower.

"I suppose," she hesitated.

"It's really nice," I insisted, and with that push she put it on and went off, a coat over the blouse.

Her family life in the South had been what Daphne considered genteel. She often quoted her father, whom she described as a gentleman fisherman, and she loved to tell the tales of events he "staged" with his family. He was a showman, by her accounts, and judging from her tirades against us for the way the house controlled her money, she had inherited some of his showman's ability.

Daphne's sense of dignity was fed by her "connections" with people outside the house. Once, when a prominent physician in her community was touring the house as a potential board member, Daphne introduced him to me with pride. She'd been his patient. She knew him!

When she told me about the gumbo her family in the South ate, I suggested that she cook it for her housemates. "I bet most of them haven't had gumbo before." I thought she might take pride in making something for her housemates—none of whom she appeared to have much respect for—if she could provide an example of southern cuisine.

"I like it with shrimp," she said.

"We'll look up a recipe. Put the ingredients you need on the week's shopping list, and you can make it." I pushed her. I was eager for her to earn a reputation in the house for being the mover and shaker that she was in the rest of her life.

I should have recognized that Daphne's assent carried elements of bluff when she began to reel off the ingredients we needed *ex tempore*. "Shrimp, celery, green pepper...."

A recipe I consulted listed an elaborate array of ingredients for that week's shopper to get at the grocery store. Oysters, crab, onions, gumbo filé...a host of rich things. The shellfish alone broke the house budget for the entire week.

All the ingredients were collected on the kitchen counter that afternoon, waiting to be put together, when Daphne claimed she had an appointment. She promised to be back in time to work with me to make the gumbo, however. But an hour before I was scheduled to go home she still had not appeared. I went into the kitchen and began chopping vegetables. My onion tears flowed freely.

The celery chopped easily. I was coming to the green pepper when Daphne appeared, her head scarf wrapped around her head askew. "I'm hungry. I didn't have time to eat anything," she said as she went to the cupboard without removing her coat and shook out a huge bowl of breakfast cereal. Having eaten that, and still wearing her coat, she offered to chop the last green pepper, which she did, seeds and all. At last, following the recipe's instructions, I put it all together and left. The broth was simmering on the stove as I went home.

"How was your gumbo?" I asked the following morning.

"I've had better. The rice was sticky." I knew Daphne hadn't cooked the rice; the staff person on-duty had. "Besides, I like it better when it only has shrimp."

Daphne's tirades against the house escalated. "I'm gonna get out of here. I want my own apartment. I get harassed here." These were her major themes. The supervisor of the house took her dissatisfaction seriously and began to make arrangements for her to visit several congregate care facilities to see if one would meet with her approval. No one having anything to do with her care felt she was capable of living in her own apartment. Daphne continued to tell me, "When I have my own apartment I'm going to invite you for a meal." Guessing that her "own apartment" was an empty hope, I said nothing.

Daphne's anger, however, continued to simmer, and one week she was said to have hit the supervisor in charge of giving out weekly funds to the residents. The following week the supervisor, feeling jittery about the "money draw," asked me to sit in as a witness when Daphne came for her money. The idea was that with a friendly person watching, Daphne might remain calm. When I stepped inside the door of the office where she sat beside the supervisor's desk, Daphne's dour, chiseled face was framed by a gray, pearl-studded cloche.

"Before I give you your money," the supervisor said in a parental tone, "I'd like an apology for the way you hit my hand last week." Her voice was jumpy.

What I heard of Daphne's reply was inarticulate growling.

"Will you apologize?" the supervisor repeated.

"Aw, all right. Gimme my money."

"I'd like an apology, Daphne."

"Gimme my money. I apologize."

"Will you say you're sorry?" Had she not heard Daphne?

"But you hit *me*," Daphne mumbled.

"I only defended myself." What the supervisor seemed to be listening for besides an apology was a promise that Daphne wouldn't hit her again.

"Aw, I apologize. Gimme my money."

The two women were at loggerheads. Neither seemed capable of hearing the other.

"Judy, what do you think?" When the supervisor turned to me a chill passed through me. What could I say? Daphne needed to be defused, and the supervisor needed to be calmed. I knew how much Daphne wanted money. The funds being withheld from her were vital to her sense of herself. Word was that the previous week, after the exchange with the supervisor which yielded no funds, Daphne had made a "homeless" sign, gone downtown, and panhandled ten dollars.

I'd heard Daphne say she was sorry, but I knew the supervisor was somehow too nervous to hear any apology. At the same time Daphne had returned to her former suggestion that the supervisor had hit her back. I recalled that when Daphne told me about the incident the previous week she had insisted that the supervisor had hit her. Who was I to believe? In this impossible situation I sensed that I should go back to plain facts. Could I distract with a question? "How much money does Daphne have left in her account for this month?"

The supervisor looked into the plastic-zippered envelope. "Eighteen dollars and thirty-four cents," she said quietly.

"I believe Daphne apologized and stretched the truth all at the same time," I mumbled. "I think she should have her money."

The supervisor ran her hand around the inside of the envelope, drew out the bills, gathered the coins, and without a word put the money into Daphne's outstretched hand.

Daphne rose from her chair, straightened her back, and strode out of the office.

Not long after this incident, Daphne told me she had a new case manager and was leaving the house. I wasn't surprised. The word was that she had accepted a place at a congregate care facility until she could get her own apartment. We on the staff of the house guessed it would be a good long time before she was able to manage her own apartment, but I said goodbye to her and extracted a promise that when she had her apartment she would invite me for a meal. Some of the zest of my work passed out of the house when Daphne was no longer living there.

A sallow-skinned, disheveled, and less dignified woman returned several months later for a visit. She looked much older. Her narrow-eyed smile was still bright, but she didn't ask me for a hug. The poem on the following page suggests what happened on the days she did ask.

Hugs

You've soured on this house and its staff,
tell us you want to live anywhere but here.
Still…you crave your hugs.
Every day early, you leave to ride the bus,
go anywhere, apply for any bogus job,
to make a gesture, to dig out of your mess,
an avalanche of mental illness.

This morning when I climbed off
the bus on one side of the road, you
waved from the stop on the other side.
We braved a melee of passing cars,
to meet in the middle. You needed
that hug so bad you grabbed it
smack in the center of the street.

DOUGLAS

But He's So Young!

IS THE ONSET of mental illness more poignant or more hopeful when it strikes a young person? Since I didn't know the answer to that question, and because I wanted to be upbeat, I decided to be hopeful when Douglas—a red-haired, unhealthy-looking young man just out of his teens who didn't really seem mentally ill—took up residence with us. The poem "To Be Homeless" reflects the turmoil he caused me during the time he was in the house. I wanted to trust him, to believe him, but steadily he made decisions I thought were folly.

In his first days in the house I was struck by two things: his pasty-faced youth, and the fact that he had a family who cared a good deal about him. The next thing that jacked up my hope for Douglas was the fact that he began to bring oil paints and canvas to the dining room table to copy photos of landscapes. He painted stiff pictures of snow-covered mountains with a certain skill.

But Douglas's difficulty emerged all too soon. One morning when I came to the house, the word was that he had gone to the arboretum the previous evening with another young man from the house. This, of course would have been quite acceptable, but they had supposedly experimented with the psychotropic effects of mushrooms. Two things made this seem disastrous: first, it was a sign that Douglas's old problem, substance abuse, had resurfaced, and secondly, he had probably been the leader when another of our residents went astray.

The first move his case manager made was to find a day-treatment substance abuse program for him, and the second was to arrange his days when he wasn't in the treatment program so that he was busy painting, sleeping, and even peeing on schedule. There

To Be Homeless

Word is that you'll be on the streets
unless you accept a treatment program.
You've decided to accept
the house's offer to turn you out.
Treatment last time turned you off.
Immune to gloom, you've
elected homelessness.

I ask where you'll go.
You have plans to live with friends,
get a flipping-hamburgers job.
My farewell gesture, a quarter,
breaks my own rule: I give you
bus fare when you promise, yes promise
to go to Narcotics Anonymous,
which meets tonight.
I trust you.

With my quarter
you ride the bus
to procure drugs.

was no empty time in which to get into mischief. When Douglas went to the library with us I discovered he was intrigued with anything about "extraterrestrials," and in addition to spending time painting, he began to spend hours on his bed, as he told me, soaring with and fantasizing about aliens who live in space. He read rapidly and went through several books. When he dropped out of the treatment program he read still more. When I asked him why he wasn't attending the treatment, he claimed the program required him to stand in front of the entire group and speak, and he couldn't do that. Then he added, "All the people there were too rowdy."

Meanwhile I came to know him better. He had a natural politeness and a refreshingly open attitude, which meant he talked readily about himself and his past. He was always willing to go on outings with us, and he never neglected to thank whoever did something for him.

One morning, when he was on kitchen cleanup while I worked with him wiping counters, I told him that I was looking for canvas for him to paint on. "I asked at Friends Meeting if anyone had canvases we could reuse for your painting."

"Thanks. I'll be needing more. Stephanie bought one of my paintings. She gave me twenty dollars for it!"

Stephanie, one of the livelier women in the house, had taken a shine to Douglas. At first he complained that he didn't like it when she followed him about. I told him I thought he should be pleased and flattered: when Stephanie clearly needed someone to care about, she had chosen him. In the end I think he decided there were some advantages to having a friend who was a good deal older than he was but who was sweet on him.

"I hope you don't mind," I confessed that morning as we worked in the kitchen, "but when I asked for the canvases I said they were to help a young man struggling to keep his addiction in check." Douglas was shocked. I think he hadn't realized I knew he had a heroin history. At the same time he seemed almost relieved to talk to me about it.

"I may be what you all call an addict, but I'm not a junkie," he said. "Addicts can control what they use. Junkie's got no control. They steal, they deal, they swoon for their drug. They gotta have it."

"Addiction's not so bad then?" I asked.

"Addiction sucks. I had some bad trips. Once I thought I was gonna die."

"There are times I'd die for popcorn," I quipped.

Nothing more was said. We finished the dishes.

About an hour later Douglas came to the office door with a scrappy fist full of used hypodermic needles in his hand, and thrust them through the door at our house nurse. "Can you get rid of these for me?"

But the stories continued. He hooked up with his friends both inside the house and out and "used." At first he was open about it, then he closed up. There was a move afoot among the staff to place Douglas in a volunteer position where he could use his skills to paint sets for an amateur theater. He wasn't enthusiastic. "I don't want to work for nothing. I want a job!"

"The best job I ever had, I got by volunteering first. They got to know me and hired me," I told him.

Doug's dream was to be a carpenter's apprentice. When he was told he'd have to have a drug-free urine test to apply, he claimed he could do that.

After his twenty-first birthday celebration he went through a long period in which he insisted he did not "use."

"I believe you," I said when he claimed he hadn't touched anything for three months. But I fudged. I wasn't sure that I believed him. The others on the staff, more used to working with addicts, were disposed to disbelieve him, and their suspicion had become contagious. I resisted mistrusting Douglas because I liked him so much. I began to think I should pull a protective glove over my heart. If I let myself become too involved, I'd be terribly let down if he couldn't lick his drug problem.

I was torn. I told Douglas I trusted him because I thought he needed someone to trust him, but at the same time I stayed ready to be proven wrong. The poem "Dilemma," opposite, suggest my ambivalence and involvement when working with Douglas.

Then, suddenly, after a spate of denials, Douglas admitted he had used.

"Once in three months! What's all the storm?"

"We don't think you understand the threat of addiction. You still think you can control it."

Dilemma

Your progress appears to have fallen apart.
You whisper to friends in the stairwell,
flaunt money in fishy ways.
Your case manager claims
a different demeanor's attacked you.

Today, like every other day, you come walking.
Your cronies come too, and spirits are high.
The darkest clouds feel light.
I drop a dour note when I introduce my
regret. "You said you'd go to Narcotics
Anonymous, but we haven't heard you did."
"I went last night. The people were all old.
But there's one in Burien Monday night.
I've heard they're younger. I'll go."
I report this news. Your case manager
frowns. "Burien's the place where his friends are."
Are you so sly as to conjure empty promises?
I wonder. Don't know, but
I'd rather be a fool than a cynic.

"You bet I can."

"I surely hope so. You're a kid with talent. It's a shame to waste it."

"My family wishes I'd stop." In his meditative tone I heard the influence of a family that cares.

"We all want you to stop and stay stopped." I said.

"I'll go Monday to NA," he promised.

Meanwhile the staff decided they'd seen too much shilly-shallying. Doug's case manager gave him the word that either he attended a treatment program or he'd be out on the streets, homeless.

Cheerfully, Doug decided to try living on the streets.

"Where will you go?" I asked him.

"I've got friends. I'll get a job flipping hamburgers."

"I just hope you're not dreaming," I said to Douglas as we walked along a waterfront path in the park. The madrona trees leaned out to spill their dark looks on us from the bank behind our path.

On the way back we stopped at a supermarket to buy something for dinner at the house, and Doug spoke to me again. "If I'm going to go to NA tonight I need a quarter for bus fare."

Residents steadily asked to borrow money from me, and always I refused to lend, let alone give, any money to anyone. This time I gave Doug a quarter to get to the meeting. We got back to the house, and Doug investigated what bus to take.

The next morning at a staff meeting Doug's case manager claimed he'd refused treatment, and decided to be homeless.

"But he did go to Narcotics Anonymous last night," I broke in.

She guffawed. "The word is he shot up in Burien last night."

He'd broken his promise. Besides that, my quarter had helped him to get heroin. I felt betrayed.

The staff meeting finished, and I rushed out to find Doug. "They laughed at me in the staff meeting when I said you'd gone to NA last night," I told him. The chagrined look on his face gave me some comfort. Conveniently, he'd forgotten until I reminded him that I had extracted a promise from him.

The next development in Doug's saga came soon after that. "I've decided to go to a live-in treatment program," he told me.

"Do you mean that? Tomorrow you won't tell me something different?"

"I mean it. I've chosen one and phoned them. Treatment will be stressful, but...."

As I listened to Doug and watched his pale face, heard his plans and promises, I realized that my faith in him had been strained out. I was far too wary now to believe he would do what he said he was going to do.

I did observe a new fact, however. He got himself a ruled notebook and began to spend hours in his room writing what he said was a book about extraterrestrials. It was as if in soaring, escaping into space, he could sabotage his move to a treatment center. He went to the library with us and checked out books on how to write fiction. I knew he read them, because he began to ask me about bits of advice he had learned from them. About this writing, he seemed in earnest. Tentatively, I rejoiced.

Doug continued to talk about going to a live-in treatment program, but nothing happened. He didn't leave the house for any live-in program, nor did he seem to be making an effort to telephone the man who could help him be admitted. When I asked him about it, he claimed he'd called but the man was unavailable.

On another walk he spoke of his fear of going to a live-in program and the stress he expected from it.

"Sure, treatment's gonna be hard! Think of the stress as a hurdle. You have to jump hurdles to reach your goal—better painting, better writing—in short, a better future," I preached to him.

"You make it sound good," he said.

I ached to have him clear that hurdle.

Two more weeks went by. I heard him occasionally making other fruitless calls to the man who was supposedly going to help him get admitted. The poem on the following page suggests Doug's ambivalence.

It was summer, and Douglas continued to lift the spirits of his housemates when he joined us, as he usually did, on our outings. He continued to lift my spirits on those outings. He cared about the other residents, respected them, was courteous to them in a way that very few of the rest were. One day in a staff meeting, when our psychiatrist said that he couldn't be sure whether Douglas really had a psychosis or whether the symptoms he showed were a result of narcotics, I began to dare to hope that his

Recurrence

You're still in the house.
You've left off painting to write
a book about extraterrestrials.
Do you escape into space
to sabotage your move to treatment?
For two weeks you've been making
useless calls to the center where
you say you want to go.
Denial dogs your resolve.

But, because you're always ready for
outings, forever upbeat about
where we go, nothing squelches
my fondness for you. You're decent.
You dream of space and soaring,
continue brushes with paint.
I ache for you to change,
to know drugs dam your dreams.
I yearn for you to ditch stagnation.

symptoms were caused by his drug use. If that were true, his psychosis might not be permanent.

Then one day, quite suddenly, a place at the residential treatment center was available to him. I came into the house one morning and Douglas was gone. He had left no special word, no goodbye, but somehow I knew he would have liked to. As with many other good things he wanted to do in his young life, he had possessed only an intention. Intention has to be enough, I told myself.

Six weeks after Douglas left the house for the treatment center he came back one weekend. I wasn't there, but he left a manuscript for me to look at. It was a handwritten, two-hundred-eighty-nine-page science fiction novel. With it was a page of handwritten questions for me to answer about my reaction to the novel. He left word that he wanted it back the following week. It was a summer week. My grandchildren were visiting, and I could snatch only a scrap of time to have a look. The book was about his beloved extraterrestrials. Yes, it was derivative; no, it was nowhere near ready for publication. But what excited me was seeing the imagination and self-discipline that had gone into making it. Was it possible Doug had given up persistence in doing drugs for persistence on this manuscript? That's not what I asked in the note I wrote him, however. I wrote him ideas that I hoped would encourage him and give him a few suggestions, trying to be strictly upbeat. I said I hoped I'd see the manuscript again.

Douglas never brought his manuscript to the house again, but six months later I sent him a Christmas card with my telephone number, and I got a phone call. "I'm out of the treatment center. I have a girlfriend, I have a job. I'm doing great," he told me. I wanted to believe him—and I did.

KEVIN

The Flip Side of Being Young

DOUGLAS'S YOUTH turned out to be on his side. By contrast, Kevin's youth made working with him more poignant. When Kevin joined us at the house, he was a large but gentle youth, one who was supported by a loving family, all of whom—his grandmother, his parents—expressed a great deal of interest in his wellbeing and progress.

According to the stories he told and the reports from his parents, Kevin led a normal boy's life with his family until he was just short of seventeen. According to his stories, he and his father fished together, and his father and mother both enjoyed hiking with him. He spoke frequently of memorable family outings—swimming, snorkeling. But after his first episode of psychosis there followed a period when stressful situations spun Kevin out of control, and his family began to suspect they might be in danger during further episodes.

Kevin's mental illness came on quickly. His family, confronted with evidence of severe mental illness, felt their world greatly altered, as his mother explains in the afterword to this book. The family came to us to see if we could receive him from the mental hospital and work with him. With medication, could he become normally active and independent again? The hope was that he could resume doing things he enjoyed on his own, that he could regain confidence in his ability to live independently.

The staff's first effort with Kevin was to help him follow through when he said he'd like to have a volunteer job. He seemed intrigued by wooden boats. Since he said he'd like to volunteer at the Center for Wooden Boats, our vocational counselor went with him to the training so as to get a sense of what might be required of Kevin. Kevin sat quietly at the training and seemed to take in the suggestions easily, but he never wanted to go to the Center for Wooden Boats again.

His next decision was to volunteer at the library. His case manager got him telephone numbers to call to explore this possibility, and he made some effort. The runaround he got when he reached beyond the phone menus to live people was daunting to this young lad. All his doubts about himself were reinforced by the response he got to his inquiries, and he gave up. He continued to enjoy trips to the library, but while he was there he wandered around without much purpose and checked out books only sometimes.

Meanwhile this clean young man made little effort to make friends with his housemates. When he could overcome his depression and get out of bed, he usually went on the walks and aquarium outings we offered. I remember how proud he was once to be able to help a housemate fasten a seat belt that had to be adjusted. On outings my chats with him as we walked were always full of his enthusiasm. They were slightly disjointed, however. Like this:

"Ever been to Heather Lake? The fishing there's great." (In his conversations he always seemed genuinely interested in me.)

"No. What kind of fish do you catch there?"

"My dad and I used to fish there. It's pretty cold for swimming."

"Puget Sound's cold for swimming as well."

"Yes, but I'd like to scuba dive. If I had a wetsuit I'd dive right in."

"We'll hold you to that when the weather's warmer."

"Can we walk out on the ferry dock?"

On the dock he took great pleasure in stopping to peer down into the clear water to look for fish. His love of nature and things natural was real. He picked up plastic can holders from six-packs when he found them on the ground because, as he said once, "they might be harmful to fish and animals who get caught in them."

Sometimes, however, his physical strength suddenly flagged. He would grow tired and have to sit and wait until we returned from our walk. On those occasions it seemed as if his mind somehow put a damper on his body. Sadly, when Kevin had been with us for about two months, we began to have more trouble getting him out of bed to join us for our walks. He seemed depressed. I told myself I'd be depressed, too, if I were facing the possibility of

You Didn't Get Better

Your bright ideas when strung
together, never make much sense.
You tell of hikes to mountain lakes,
your dad, who clearly cares for you, but....
Begrudging, you rise from bed at noon
with no verve for anything but candy bars.

Our doctor persuades
you to try a miracle medication.
Your mask burns brighter,
you walk farther, your quick ideas
come back. But like Sisyphus,
each morning your stone's
at the bottom of the trail
to that clear mountain lake.

a debilitating mental illness for the rest of my life. The poem on the opposite page suggests my sense of Kevin's state.

In part because Kevin spoke of enjoying swimming, we arranged a regular swimming time each week, and the poem "The Unbearable Lightness of Water," on the following page, reflects his love of swimming.

Psychiatric medications sometimes exacerbate weight problems, and Kevin gained weight. He almost always wanted to go with us on outings, but he often hung back, tired. "Death March" describes the way his weight handicapped him.

Kevin frequently phoned his grandmother, and often took the bus to visit her, but he seemed uninterested in friendships he might form with his housemates. He also seemed untempted by their drug-using follies. But a young man with no friends is lonely. The poem "Volunteering?" suggests the poignancy of his loneliness.

When Kevin moved to a house near our treatment center he was able to get along with his new roommate, whom another lad had needed to get away from by simply learning to pass him heedlessly. His family frequently arranged for Kevin to come home for a week at a time, and he spent many nights with his grandmother. Outings continued to be more enjoyable when Kevin went with us.

One afternoon, on a summer outing, a storm broke and rain poured down. We were beside Puget Sound, and Kevin, riding shotgun, looked out at a passing ferry. "What time does your ferry go?"

"Four-forty," I said. "Gotta get back to the house quick, walk up for my bus."

"But its raining."

"Yeah, I'll run."

"Here, take this." He pulled a pouch with a folded raincoat from his coat pocket, one he had intended to use himself on the walk home.

I accepted. "I'll bring it back next week."

"Just fold it carefully again."

Feeling cared about, protected, I went off to my bus stop.

The Unbearable Lightness of Water

I knock and shove your door open
to find you splat out sleeping. "Kevin!" I say,
"Our swims start today. You need to get up,
get breakfast, your meds, be ready at noon."
At 11:00 I knock again. "Yes," you mutter, "I'll go."
At 11:45 I knock. "Fifteen minutes till we go."
You slouch to the door, "Kinda short notice."
"I've called you twice already."
You rise, descend on the kitchen,
pick up a poppy seed muffin, and say,
"I'm tired. I won't go."
"But this swimming deal's for you.
Come anyway. If you're tired
you can watch the rest of us."
"Should I bring a towel?" "Yes."
I hear you say what you don't say:
See what my mind has done to me?

At the pool you climb in, grab
a spongy noodle, float on it,
splash, dunk, swim, and come alive.
Deep below me, my foot kicks a leg
and you pop up surprised.
You balk at leaving when it's time.
When I coax you to leave your
bed next week, will your mind give you
what your flesh needs?

Death March

I announce an open-air saltwater pool, and
you're game to go. But you begin to doubt
when we wander lost on crisscross paths in the park.
At last we find the noisy pool.
You brave the children's shouts, and frolic
(for you, frolic means one kick of your huge leg)
in the lightness the salt lends
until you're cool,
then quit.

Leaving, there looms a wooded
rooted path up to the van.
You leer and dub the climb a "death march."
Halfway up you mumble, "I think I might pass out."
I panic. What would I do,
with your huge frame splat
out on the dusty path?
I tell you, "Time, we have."
You pause, stare straight ahead, don't crumple.

Halting, you move those chubby legs
till the hilltop stumbles up.
Next swim, I decide against that pool
before you say, "No more death marches."
Of late, each step you take
looms a small death.

Volunteering?

After swimming we go to the library.
You check out a video,
In the Company of Wolves.
I ask what you've done to follow up
on what you said you wanted to do—
volunteer at the library. You rarely fail
to find a frail excuse.

"Make the phone call," I plead.
"Lets see the video," you propose,
preferring to watch wolves
when there's someone
to watch with you. While we watch
you ask, "How are your new shoes working out?"
In the lonely world of mental illness, you
care enough to ask about my shoes.

TAYLOR AND RUDY

Where's Their Mental Problem?

TAYLOR

THE HOUSE HAD its lion and its lamb: two young men whose behavior seemed to be more connected to their chronic physical problems than to their mental problems. The body and mind are so intricately intertwined that in the case of these two men I found it impossible to separate what was the effect of a mental instability and what was the result of a physical problem. Was this because medications regulated both their mental and physical problems? I could wonder, but I hadn't the training to know.

Taylor was the lion, Rudy the lamb. My introduction to Taylor came when I overheard another volunteer speaking with him about menus for the house. One of our aims was to train residents to do their own menu planning. I overheard Taylor speaking the praises of eggplant and recommending that we make ratatouille because a vegetarian diet is healthiest. "Now, there's a sophisticated young man," I noted to myself.

"Mohawk," on the following page, describes the one moment in my year of working in the house when I had any sense of physical threat. Still, at the same moment I saw Taylor thrust his fist out, I felt he didn't hit me because he couldn't let himself. He retained a shred of control over his anger. The poem's depiction of that momentary scrape with violence makes tame drama! Taylor was a complicated man, and most of his anger was expressed verbally in complaints; but those, too, because he was so soft-spoken, remained undramatic. He spoke myriad accusations, but his demeanor was usually low-key. He voiced his irritations, but he usually didn't act them out, except perhaps to transform them into

Mohawk

Scrupulous, daily, you shave your Mohawk.
Sullen moods now hold your spirit hostage.
A brute disease has just begun to stalk.

You speak defiance in your very walk.
You choose your clothes to fit the latest fads.
Scrupulous, daily, you shave your Mohawk.

"Why not do drugs?" you ask, knowing the chalk
of death cannot be changed obeying laws,
and brute disease has now begun to stalk.

You rap in rhythm, boast you know all rock,
wear shades to mask your bloodshot, angry eyes.
Scrupulous, daily, you shave your Mohawk.

Hungry at lunch, you strike the freezer lock
and thrust a fist at me before you stop.
Scrupulous, daily you shave your Mohawk.
Your brute disease has just begun to stalk.

aggressive skateboarding. Sometimes he went with us to a beachfront where there was a bicycle path that he could use for skateboarding. While the rest of us moseyed along, Taylor, sweat shining on his torso, would fly past us on his skateboard, hoping to glean our admiration.

Good moods made Taylor pleasant to talk to. He posed as a rock music aficionado and claimed to know a great deal about all kinds of popular music. He hankered after, and told me he was badgering his father for, a set of drums with which to become an expert drummer. His family, although they gave him support, didn't appear to include drums as part of what they wanted to do for him.

When I first knew Taylor he expressed an interest in having a job. Our vocational adviser helped him get one in a trendy men's clothing store. But he held it for only a brief period before he was back at the house, out of a job. To take orders was difficult for Taylor. He blamed his failure on the store owners, of course.

Taylor began to act in ways that made us suspect he was using drugs. Each day he wore a new outfit in the latest style—different clothes selected daily to fit his Mohawk haircut. What didn't fit this stylishness was his SSI allowance. How did his meager allowance sustain such expenditures? One morning I sat in a staff meeting thinking how Taylor had admitted he wanted to do drugs. Clearly, he got some kind of thrill from playing with the forbidden. Considering that he knew he probably didn't have long to live anyway, I had some sympathy for his choice to use. What I did question was whether he was dealing drugs. Drug-dealing was another matter, since it could contribute to crippling others. The poems on the next two pages suggests some of the details of Taylor's life at the house.

Taylor was easier to get along with when he moved from our house to one two doors away. His new independence seemed to set him up.

Taylor didn't go to San Francisco as he hoped to, as described in the poem "Bouyancy," even for a week. He settled into living independently in his "supported living" house, coming to the main house each day for his medications, and living life the way he wanted to live it. His roommate was an irritation to him, but he coped

Buoyancy

You are softer lately. Your speech
is low-voiced, gentler. Something better
floats your boat. Your anger's cooped up,
but nothing calms your illness.

Four of your hats were stolen last week.
Certain who's the culprit, you seem
resigned to losing them, and still you
daily change your dapper clothes.
Each day a heavy chain hangs across your
baggy pants like a long watch fob.
Your shoulders shine beneath
a tank top. Yes, you're right in style.
Something floats your boat.

What you call promoting (drug-dealing?)
must fund your fancy dressing.
You come in late and refuse U.A.'s.
Why would you reject a test if you
were not a user? Still, you promise
as bribe for a Frisco trip
whole buckets of pee.
I hope you do the right thing,
but if you'd rather be happy than right,
who am I to question?
It's your life.
Buoyant, your boat floats
as you sail out to die.

Housewarming

"Fresh starts are what moves give you."
You've wanted to leave this house for months,
and now your new house boasts fir floors
and you have wind beneath your wings.
To adorn floors with scatter rugs,
to hang house plants for greenery,
to sleep in a double bed graced with a spread
(In evidence only when you make your bed)
are signs of wind in your wings.

Moving day's a downer. Grease-caked dishes
wait beside the filthy sink. Catsup spots
the cupboards bloody. You turn gentle,
thank me, when I begin to wash the dishes, but
there's no wind beneath your wings
till you decide to fly. You scrape,
sponge, clean, make counters,
cupboards shine. When you finish, leave,
you tell your housemate "Clean the bathroom!" and…
your wind stirs beneath *his* wings, and…
he does.

with that mess as well. Eventually he was able to move to yet another nearby house that we rent to clients under our care. Miraculously, neither Taylor's mental or physical health showed signs of deterioration. For the time being, he was one of the stalwarts the supervisor in "Growing Solutions" could count on to carefully pick and use good taste in making up a lettuce mix for the restaurants to which we sell.

From Taylor's viewpoint one of the best things that happened to him was finding a slightly damaged drum for sale for five dollars. The damage didn't effect the sound, and he could drum away.

RUDY

Rudy's a boyish, lethargic man with a heart problem. When I first came to the house he was said to be getting ready for heart surgery. But he didn't have surgery. When I asked him about it later he said, "I decided not to," and I didn't question him further. What was clear about Rudy's physical condition was that he was obese and moved slowly. Because I was so fond of him, I tried not to think about how hard it was on his heart to pump his life-blood around his huge frame.

Word was that Rudy had been a high school hockey star. His first mental break had come in high school when, as he told me, he was under "peer pressure"—he was seventeen and going to pick up a girl for a date. It was hard now to think he had ever moved rapidly enough to be adept at sports, and it is easy to imagine that sports put another kind of pressure on him that his heart and mind weren't up to—to move fast. The life must have gone out of him when he shed his last bright-colored hockey jersey. Did he leave it limbless and crumpled on his bedroom floor?

Lucky for Rudy's friends, his kind nature didn't disappear with his energy. Rudy was always willing to go to the hospital with us to visit other residents, to show other people in small ways that he cared. He was helpful with things like pumping gas when we arrived at a self-serve station in the van. His life was dull, however, and I guessed he went on outings with us as much for something to do as because the walking was good for him. He was good to have with us, particularly because, although he was always slow, he was someone who could be counted as a steady presence. In any group he would act calmly, sanely.

On election day Rudy was proud of the reason he couldn't go walking with us. He was instead going off to help one of the mayoral candidates. I believe his father, who lived nearby, had persuaded him to work for his favorite candidate on election day. I had previously encouraged Rudy to find volunteer work, but it hadn't happened until that day. That one day, however, he was enthusiastic enough about what he was doing to say to me, "You oughta come and help!"

Considering the letdown he must have experienced after his early successes, Rudy had every reason to be angry at life. Instead he sought out a group that promoted "inner peace." One day I was at the bus stop reading and waiting. My book was just suggesting that "love is a force, not a result," when Rudy got off a bus and we began to wait at the bus stop together. "Where you been?" I asked him.

"Downtown, talking with a woman from the Inner Peace Society."

"Did she have inner peace?" I asked.

"She seemed to. You seem to."

Was it his comment? My reading? Something drove me to preach. "I think I've found the secret of inner peace for me—being useful. My father was useful up until the last few weeks before he died. When he lost the strength to be useful to anybody, he willed his heart to fail and died."

Thinking about what I'd said, I realized I'd spoken in the hope that Rudy would find some volunteer post outside the house and gain pride of being of use to somebody. I decided later, however, that it's enough to have Rudy useful to me as a steady, cheerful, though lethargic presence on our outings.

The poignancy of his physical and mental decline, however, remained as "Nostalgia" suggests.

Rudy also had his dreams, as the poem "Faithful One" suggests. But he was hardly tenacious about achieving them.

Nostalgia

Seven of us drive to a park to walk.
We go past your old school and you gawk
at children on the playground. "I'm no fool,"
you say, "voted me 'outstanding
student' in sixth grade at that school!"

At Lincoln Park, Kevin has to pee
right off, and we wait on the sidewalk,
blocked in rigid squares. You and Peter
play—lunge at each other's Buddha
bellies, bounce your bodies
off each other—a jab at martial arts,
complete with grunts.
The fight alarms until we see it's only show.
Your meds stifle stormy scuffling
except for moments like today
when like two kids on a playground you pound in your fond feelings.

Faithful One

Today no one wants to do
anything. You are the only one
who chooses to walk till Willie
changes his mind and we go.
Our path stretches along the Sound.
We use the shoreline to dream on.
When air and sunlight tickle my nose,
I prepare a punchy question:
"Choose where you'd
be in six months, what
you'd dream of doing?"

"At camp in Iowa. My Peace
Church buddies hang out there.
Maybe at work...
whatever chance comes."

This clear-aired day, your dreams
may not be clearheaded,
but does it matter?

MYRTLE

An Awakening

MYRTLE WAS A placid, silent fixture in the house when I first started. She spent whole days in silent domination of the living room from her prone position on the couch. She stirred herself for a cigarette once an hour, or nosed into the dining room to beg some when the smell of someone else's popcorn permeated the living room, but basically she spent her days dozing on the couch. At night she often had incontinence problems, and occasionally she had them by day. Each morning she rose, appeared at the med window for her medications, asked for her cigarette (which was given her each hour on the hour only after she assured us she had been to the bathroom), and returned to the living room to snooze. Why did she choose the living room rather than her own bedroom? Did she like company, even while dozing? Did she not like her bedroom? Did she sleep purposely where others might hear her cough and be concerned? I could only guess. No one asked her questions because we did not expect answers. Myrtle was forthcoming with only a few words. What we heard from her all that first autumn that I worked at the house was a persistent, hacking cough, and that concerned us.

I came to expect little more of Myrtle than to be a soft pillow of a couch potato who rarely acknowledged anyone else's presence. Since she showed no interest in going on outings, we seldom invited her. But the fact that she emerged from her bedroom to sleep seemed significant. Was it a gesture toward acknowledging that she was in a community? She spoke to the staff only occasionally, and almost never to her housemates. Without making eye contact, she answered questions put to her, or spoke to ask for a cigarette, food, or her meds. What she said was always in truncated phrases. We knew her snore better than we knew her speaking voice.

Myrtle did do her part. Faithfully each week she signed up for chores, and gained a reputation as being the most thorough dish-washer in the house. Thorough meant that she ran hot water over the dishes for long periods, rinsing them to make them ready for the dishwasher. Never did she stop up the sink and collect soapy water to wash with. Thorough also meant that she wiped the counters with a certain gusto.

I took pleasure whenever I could say honestly, "Good job, Myrtle."

Her reply was always a flat "Thank you."

The day after Thanksgiving Myrtle must have caught the holiday mood. When we proposed a walk in Lincoln Park, she was willing to go. Since Myrtle was usually so inactive, we were delighted that she would come along and did not insist that she change her clothes. She braved the chilly weather wearing red gym shorts and bare bow-legs. The November sun made long Seattle shadows on the path that ran beside the sea. Reflection off the water augmented the autumn light. A number of holiday walkers took the air with us, and several times Myrtle lifted a hand in a jagged gesture of greeting to those she passed. We walked on a path beside the sea. Her long, tousled hair rippled and curled around her face like Botticelli's painting of Venus rising from the sea on a shell. Our Venus, having a number of pounds on Botticelli's, might have sunk the shell.

We came to a fork in the path. Each person was asked to choose which path he or she wanted to explore on the way back, but warned that one route was a good deal longer. Myrtle chose to take the shorter route. "I'll go with Judy," she said. I was thrilled to hear her utter one of the longest sentences I had heard her speak. Besides, she had called me by name!

It was as if delight had invaded Myrtle. Returning on the path beside the sea, she continued to gesture with one hand at passers-by as seven of us straggled along the path in an uneven line. Suddenly she grabbed Mike's arm and muttered, "Buddy system." Neither Mike nor Myrtle had been on an outing for weeks, and the cold air must have invigorated them. They began to sing.

Having heard only a snippet of their song, I caught up with

Myrtle's pigeon-toed lope to ask, "When did you learn that song you sang?"

"Wrote it, a long time ago," she said, dropping Mike's hand and continuing at a good clip.

By the time we reached our van Myrtle was tired, but she plunked herself into a seat and began to sing a second song, a love song. That tune finished, she uttered a single word, "Discombobulate."

"That's a favorite word of mine. Where did you hear it?"

"My mother invented it a long time ago," she said, fastening her seat belt.

Silence followed. After a long pause she said, "I had a whale of a time."

"That's good, I hope you'll go again." I said.

"No, I'm too tired."

Christmas—a difficult time in the house—was coming. Those who had families, went home to them of course, but most of our residents didn't have people who cared about them to go to at Christmas. We tried to build a sense of community for those who were there with a gift exchange and a special meal. Everyone who decided to participate drew a name. Then we gave each person ten dollars and took them shopping to select a gift for the person whose name they had drawn.

Myrtle selected red nail polish and drugstore gold earrings for the woman whose name she had drawn. We spread all the Christmas wrappings out on the pool table in the game room, and people came in one at a time to wrap their gifts. When Myrtle came I discovered she had considerable dexterity. Some of the other wrappings were uneven and crumpled, but Myrtle's job was both neat and decorative after she had help cutting her small pieces of wrapping paper. She behaved like an enthusiastic child with the scotch tape, liberally smearing the small package with it.

Six of us went together to buy a small scrubby tree, the cheapest at Chubby and Tubby's. When it was graced with ornaments—fuzzy, faded red runners, no lights—anticipation built. When they had wrapped their gifts, everyone was invited to put their packages under the decorated tree. Several packages were under the tree when our program supervisor spoke a word of caution. "There's been stealing in the house. Maybe it's unwise to put the gifts out and in sight under the tree so many days before Christmas."

"In the spirit of Christmas, who would swipe a Christmas gift?" I muttered to myself. But I was green. I decided I'd better think about what to do to prevent thefts. When I consulted the program director, he had a good idea: "Let them own their gifts," he said. "Tell each person there's a risk of their gift being stolen if its left under the tree, and ask them if they want it hidden or left out."

I did that. Nine people wanted their gifts left under the tree. Two people couldn't take that kind of risk. We hid their gifts, and for Christmas morning I told the staff where they were. A pile of wrapped presents on the floor beneath the tree added anticipation and excitement to the day.

"Since Myrtle chose to leave her gift in place, that must mean she'll leave the others there," I said to the program director.

"Myrtle stole from her own roommate. Don't count on it."

I felt inexperienced, naïve. Still, I habitually jump off figurative cliffs expecting to deal with the consequences only at the bottom. I had encountered another precarious moment, and arranged to leave gifts under the tree.

Christmas came. The gift exchange took place. The day after Christmas one small packet, Myrtle's gift for Daphne, who'd gone home, remained unwrapped and lonely under the tree. I saw the gift Myrtle had chosen and wrapped lying under the tree—red nail polish—and remembered that Myrtle liked nail polish herself. In fact, she loved to paint her chubby, bitten nails. Now her nails were pale, and the nail polish was still under the tree. Inside, I grinned all over.

All through that winter I continued to be delighted each rare time Myrtle decided to go with us on one of those house outings. The poem "Awakening," on the following page, depicts what sometimes happened.

One morning Myrtle sat stiffly on a straight wooden chair for perhaps three minutes with her mouth gaping open as if it were frozen that way. "What's happening?" I asked.

"I'm aerating my esophagus," she said, staring straight ahead, her eyes bulging, her bulbous breasts sagging. That afternoon, although I couldn't persuade her to come to the library with us, I brought her back a video to watch.

Awakening

The sky glares pink flame as I ride the ferry home,
though the clouds wear black edges.
You put fire in my heart
when you chose to walk with us today.
I rambled with you, talked with you
as I would with any woman.
Winterized people taking the air cluttered
Alki beach on this clear, cold day.
Your breasts bounced as you clipped along,
your legs showed hairy below your shorts.
Two small girls, hands over their mouths,
stared. You failed to notice. I did.
The fire fades, black brush strokes against the blue.

"It's a classic comedy, the Marx Brothers, *A Day at the Races*," I told her as I put it on. Two housemates joined her in the living room to watch it. At first Myrtle seemed anything but absorbed, but then she began to chuckle in appropriate places as slapstick humor animated the black-and-white screen.

The film went on for an hour and forty-five minutes, during which time Myrtle left to eat her lunch. Her housemates had long since grown bored and left. She returned as the screen blossomed with a dance, and pushed herself back in her chair to sing. Not the songs on the screen, but others that fit the horse-race rhythms. Then, when the race rose to a climax, Myrtle rose as well. No Al Jolson, knee to the ground, for her. She planted herself three feet in front of the screen, her legs out, her plump arms clawing the air, her body making a huge X. She held that pose for several minutes until the film ended. Her whole squashed spirit seemed to burst out.

One of Myrtle's favorite trips that winter was to the aquarium. The poem on the next page suggests how she would come alive seeing sea life.

Swimming was where we discovered how much Myrtle loved water. Because so many of our residents needed exercise I requested and received a reduced rate at a local pool where I could take them each week to swim. From my own swimming exercise class I collected used swimming suits, and gathered a group of about six people for our first venture to the pool. Myrtle said she'd like to go, but when we had adjusted the straps of her suit and arrived at the pool's edge, she could not be coaxed down the stairs into the water. She was too frightened. She said she had cracked her head once.

She continued to go with us for three weeks, despite her fright, because she liked to sit in the spa with the warm water swirling about her.

By the third week those of us who went into the pool had developed a ritual that included "Marco Polo." This is a game where the person who is "It" closes his or her eyes. Then he or she calls out "Marco" and everyone else must call "Polo," letting the person know by sound where they are. It's a lively game. Rarely could we get anyone to play it according to the rules—actually keeping their eyes shut—but we yelled and splashed and played anyway. During

Find the Green, the Blue

A winter day. You lie on the
couch unmoving, except to cough,
in a skirt too dirty to wear
anywhere. "Come with us to the

aquarium," I say, and you
change to a pair of shorts, and I
insist they're wrong for the weather.
At length you find long pants because

you really want to go see fish.
Eight free tickets ease our entry.
"See the fish on your own, and we'll
meet," I say to four who are "capable."

You and two others stick with me.
Our two brash buddies frighten skit-
tery visitors, so I'm involved
finessing "unrulies," while your

delight burgeons. You begin to
float like the undulating fish.
Intrigue with an anemone
fringe, a sea cucumber spike, wipes
out the dead affect you came with.
Your spread-fingered hands flutter at
each window where bright fish flash. You
persist, hunt out the green, the blue
you didn't know you came for.

this game on her third time at the pool, I noticed Myrtle poised at the top of the steps she had so feared, clearly contemplating coming into the pool. At my next glance she was in the pool. Without fuss or praise, I went to her and calmly offered her a foam "noodle" to help her float. She didn't want to play our game, but she did begin splashing about, with the noodle across her chest keeping her afloat. Clearly the water felt good, and she began bobbing about, unafraid of movement.

We had finished our game when I noticed that Myrtle and her noodle were drifting into water too deep for her to touch bottom. Unaware that she couldn't touch bottom, she was nonetheless close to the side of the pool. I kept an eye on her. Suddenly she was floundering and I heard her call, "Help me!" She had lost her grip on her float-sponge. I started toward her, but before I could get there a lifeguard had quietly reached down, offered her a hand, and suggested she pull herself hand over hand to shallower water, gripping the side of the pool. This she did, and everyone including Myrtle stayed calm. She left the pool by the steps and went to the spa.

"Darn," I thought to myself. "We'll never get her back in the pool now!" No good to try to coax. Best to leave her alone. Five minutes later she came down the steps and into the pool again.

Myrtle became our most faithful swimmer. Others came and went, but Myrtle always chose to go. Yet only once could we get her to play tag with us. She developed a ritual: using the floats she paddled back and forth on a twenty-foot course in one corner of the pool. Once she went with us to an outdoor saltwater pool, but since there were no steps to help her get in, only a ladder, I could not persuade her to swim. Instead she plunked herself down on a chaise lounge for a sunbath.

Since her bathing suits were not new, they didn't last long, and with tears and stretching she went through two. Finally we helped her buy a new one that fit, and when she was wearing it Kevin commented to me that she looked very nice. "Tell her that," I said.

"Myrtle," he yelled across the pool, "Your new suit's nice."

"Thank you," she said in her usual flat tone, not loud enough for him to hear.

That day she paddled happily in the pool long after the others had gone to the spa. On the way home in the van she sang along with all the songs on the radio. Her listening housemates raised their eyebrows. They were unaware that Myrtle even knew so many words, let alone could sing them. When we arrived home and parked the van, a chorus of thank-yous rang out from all the swimmers, Myrtle included. Then she added, "I had a whale of a time."

Because all our residents who want to help with cooking need to pass a public health food-handler's test, we tutor them with a practice test and accompany them to the office where they take the test. When we had put it off as long as possible, we persuaded Myrtle and Carol to take the test.

On the day we were to go, I arrived at the house to find Myrtle in bed, ready to go, with her clothes on. Carol, who'd been eager to go, had decided she couldn't. "I'll go grocery shopping instead," she assured me, as if that switch was relevant. I knew Carol had studied well and could undoubtedly pass the test, but I also knew it was no good coaxing her. Myrtle and I got ready, and by the time we actually left, Carol had decided to go with us.

I glanced at the man behind the desk at the testing place. Was he apt to be flexible? "We're from a licensed mental health center," I said. "Our clients do their own cooking. We supervise. To do that they must, by law, pass this test. Since they work under a handicap, may I work with her?" I nodded my head at Myrtle; I felt Carol could manage on her own. Calmly, without saying yes, the man indicated that we should sit in a set of chairs set aside for study. We settled in, Myrtle next to me, Carol on the other side of her. Myrtle and I started working at the test, whispering, but after one page she seemed annoyed at the help and said, "I'll do it myself."

As I stopped working with Myrtle, Carol slipped into the chair on the other side of me. "I can't do it. I'm suffering."

"Fine, you can do it later," I said, picking up her pencil and making some choices. After I whispered three choices aloud, she took the pencil from me.

"I can't concentrate," she whined, but she went on reading questions and speaking answers aloud for me to correct. Mostly she was right. When the last page was finished, I suggested she take the test to the man behind the desk for grading.

Myrtle hadn't finished. She was mumbling and marking. When I finally saw her make the last mark I suggested she turn in her test.

The man pretended to study the results before he said, "You both passed. That will be sixteen dollars."

I pulled the cash from the envelope I had brought and said, "Thank you for your humanity," to the man and looked for his response. His poker face spoke nothing.

The elevator that took the three of us down must have sensed our pride. Our relief was palpable. I decided we had to celebrate. We went across to Starbuck's and bought expensive, fancy coffees.

More and more, when Myrtle went on outings she seemed alive and "with us." She loved the shopping outings, and haunted the perfume counters enjoying the scents. She was persuaded to join a woman's group in the house, and when the group took turns relating their ideas and feelings, what Myrtle said each time it was her turn to speak was "I like swimming." The two poems on the following page detail some of her reactions to water.

More and more, as Myrtle entered into activities at the house, her housemates began to acknowledge her as part of the community.

Water's Water

You like water, so when four of us go
to an outdoor saltwater pool you go too.
But the pool has no steps to help you in.
"I can't," you claim and stop.
Fear keeps you at the top of the ladder.
Instead you spread on a lounge,
sunbathe, give not one glance
to where we swim.

In the shower afterward, as water
slithers over your nakedness, you spatter soap
as you scramble your mouse-blonde hair.
For the uphill walk, water has freed
your cackle. You climb back to the top
breathing in puffs, call it
"The longest walk I ever took,"
and shout "hallelujah" while
beating a path to the van.

To Belong, a Water Step

We count on a game in the pool for a mixer.
But you forever choose to paddle on your own.
You sing to yourself, purr with your gravelly voice,
and when we say, "Wanta play?" always shake your head.

But today you played. Without asking, staff tagged you.
You refused to be "It" when caught, but in between
three times when you got tagged you dashed through the water
with panache, cackling, splashing, catching a housemate.
With verve and water steps, you moved to join the world.

ALAN

The Balloon that Bobbed "Get Well"

MELLOW MANNERED, dull voiced, gentle. That was my impression of Alan when I first met him as a returnee to the house. He had lived there before, been helped to find a job, and gone out on his own in an apartment. He was now coming back because, living on his own, he had probably taken his medications only irregularly and found the pressure of his job debilitating. He had had another psychotic episode, and it was decided that he again needed the stability of a supportive living community. He settled in quietly, hoping our vocational counselor would help him find another job that would have less pressure. She agreed to help, securing him a part-time job at a small pizza place.

My fondness for Alan was cemented one day when I was rolling out cookie dough. I had enlisted Delano to help me, and in the middle of the process Delano had suddenly up and left. There I was, left to finish making cookies myself! Of course I could finish them on my own. But I hadn't started to make them just to produce homemade cookies! Underlying any project I started in the house was the goal of involving the residents. My reason for volunteering was to promote activities that gave residents a sense of either pleasure or usefulness. If I finished cutting out the cookies myself and decorated them without help from anyone, that aim was foiled.

Alan rescued me. He appeared at the kitchen door and asked if I wanted help. When I said I did, we worked together. I muddled through rolling out the dough and, lamb-like, Alan wielded the cookie cutters with his clumsy fingers to create hearts and crescents. I colored sugar crystals with food coloring, and he wielded a spoon to sprinkle them over the cookies. We became a bumbling, chuckling twosome until our creations emerged edible. They tasted good.

One morning I became aware of how quickly Alan could become attacked by delusions when he forgot to take his medications. The word professionals used for what happened to him when he missed his meds was "escalation." That morning when I came in he got up from watching television in the living room and began to fish in his pants pocket. "I wrote the president to see if he can stop the takeover of this country by terrible men," he said, pulling out a crumpled piece of paper. "Will you help me send it?"

"I'll help you finish writing it, if you want," I said, "after you've had your meds. Have you had them yet this morning?"

"I don't think so."

"Why don't we get them, then?" I suggested and, docile, Alan followed me to the med window. Nimbly he tossed his head back and swallowed the meds. Then I found an excuse to do something else for the next few minutes, and Alan did not return to ask for help with his letter to the president. I could only hope that the effect of his meds had erased some of the fear I had seen in him.

One day, after Alan had been with us long enough for me to be terribly fond of him, he said to me, "Judy, did you hear? I found out yesterday that I have cancer."

"Oh, no," I said. "What did they tell you you're going to have to do?"

"Don't know yet. They want a bunch of tests, I guess."

So a new effort began to lend support to one of our residents who faced a life-threatening disease. And it didn't get easier. As Alan faced it, however, we noticed that his mental problems seemed to fade, and he seemed quite sane most of the time.

The tests revealed that there was next to nothing that could be done about Alan's cancer at the stage it had reached. Alan was going to have to play a dreadful waiting game. He might well be in and out of the hospital for help in maintaining his equilibrium while he played that game, but there was no way he could win the wait. The staff knew before he did that his cancer was incurable, and we were warned not to speak to him about his condition until the doctor had told him. Then Alan became so ill he had to be hospitalized, and we began a series of visits to him in the hospital. His housemates closed around him, expressing their caring in idiosyncratic ways. The poem "Homecoming," on the following page, suggests the scene when we brought him back home.

A week after his homecoming Alan asked to go to the grocery store with us on our weekly shopping trip. I looked at his pale, whiskered face and decided I should let him judge his own strength and not decide for him that he might have a tough time. His hair was tangled, uncombed. I didn't ask him to comb it. When we arrived at the parking lot outside Safeway, I grew jumpy. What if his stamina gave out in one of the grocery aisles? Would his breath catch in his chest? Would he have some terrible coughing spasm?

"Here's the van key. If you tire, you can come back and wait for the rest of us in the van."

Alan shrugged and didn't take the key. Instead he came with us to help choose plums. After that he fetched a bag of pears, then decided he'd find tea bags for himself.

"Don't much like the tea at the house," he said as he left to check out his own item.

When the other three of us finished and left the store, Alan was sitting outside sipping a cup of coffee he'd bought. On the way home he sat in the coveted shotgun seat. The day was warm. I pointed to an old man on the street whose layered clothes and beard hung full off him. "He must be stifling hot!"

Alan only glanced rapidly at the man before his eyes shifted to a young girl on the same street some distance away. "Look at those hot pants," he crooned.

"Ah, yes, you're a guy. You'd rather look at a girl," I quipped.

"I gotta get me a girl," he said, suddenly serious.

To that I could find nothing to say. He had girl housemates, but they didn't seem to see him in "that way." I could only wish they would.

Alan continued to spend quiet days at home without much interest in outings. At night, particularly, he began to have trouble breathing, even with the oxygen that was delivered to the house for him. When he was up and lying about, his housemates were not sure how they could express their caring. Nonetheless they hovered respectfully. At length it became necessary to transfer Alan to a nursing home better equipped to handle his breathing

Homecoming

Today you're due to be discharged.
Seven of your housemates come with me
in the van to bring you home.
Brewster, whose steady hand can steer the van,
comes along for backup.
Samantha, who loves to shop,
yearns to buy for you a
balloon that reads, "get well."
Rudy moves his slow frame faster
to show me where your room is.

You wait in your doorway
puffy-cheeked, dressed,
knees apart, hands hanging.
The nurse makes you ready
to go with care and oxygen.
Three of us crush round your wheelchair
in an elevator to descend
to the lounge where Samantha
waits, batting the balloon about.
Gentle Brewster bats back with decorum
while four others sit slouched,
waiting to lay eyes on you.

A nurse pushes you through the polished
hall, hunched-happy in your wheelchair,
balloon bobbing above you,
your motley, seven-dwarf family
strung out behind you.

At the elevator door the boost your family
gives you means you tear the tubes from your nose,
clutch the oxygen tank, rise up, and walk.
The tank hangs off you like a third arm.
Hi ho, hi ho, it's off to home we go
in the rattling van where we
give you the shotgun seat to
celebrate snatching you back.
For how long?

Fresh News

The doctor told you yesterday:
You have six months to live.
You heard and faltered home,
A waiting place to die.

Your housemates when they heard the news,
swarmed round like honeybees
afraid to giggle near you
for fear they'd leave a sting.

This morning you showered, washed your hair,
shaved your bristled cheek, and
asked to go to the bank.
When I could not take you,

You faced me, took both my hands to
say, "I love you, Judy."
What answer except "I love
you, too?" I do, but...

What is this love I feel for you?
When I'm aware that joy has so
rarely hatched from your dreams, ache
lurks in my love for you.

difficulties. At that point small brigades of his housemates paid him frequent, awkward, visits. Until there was a night in which he died quietly.

At about the same time a dear friend of mine was also battling cancer. The poem that concludes this chapter suggests the difference in the way I thought about them.

Grief Compounded

In two of my friends a cancer rages.
The one a grace-full caring mother,
the other a cared-for, brain-flawed man.

To pray about them, not for them,
I drop to my knees in the garden.
The bulbs I plant enter the earth dead
but spring will make them sprout and bloom.
Who's to say if either friend
will ever see them flower?

Their cancers may grow, their cancers may go
Hope is the job for each of them.
A faithful life replete with love
Prepares the mom for hope,
but illness leaves the man bereft
of fertile skills for living.
The one will die and leave a chasm.
The other's known so many deaths
this death is just one more.

COMMUNITY

We're Not One Big Happy Family, But....

A SENSE OF community among our residents came to be my principal goal, and outings were my chief instrument for building it. Outings in the world appeared to build the feeling that, as motley a group as we were, we were all connected in a quirky, tight way. The world outside both isolated and entertained us. By contrast, when we did things together at home, such as playing games, it was harder to ignore the other housemates who roamed about our game table as if the game were not going on. Indeed, sometimes when everyone was housebound it could feel like our very housemates were the outside world. By contrast, when a group of us piled into the van, we somehow became a group facing the world together. As a body, we could disregard odd looks, rude remarks, or any jolt we might get from being out of tune with our culture.

Picnics in which we took walks, trips to the science center, trips to the aquarium, visits to museums where we could go as a group, all helped to add color to life in the house. Varied as our problems were, when we were out together we began to feel we were all in the same boat.

To affirm our sense of community I had only to look at the difference in the caring we were able to show when a "crisis guest" arrived in the house. From time to time when people case-managed by other mental health centers came to crisis points they were sent to our house for respite of a week or less, which meant their case managers could avoid sending them to a mental hospital. Our job was to give them a break from whatever stress they were experiencing in their lives by changing their milieu. "Crisis guests" were seldom with us long enough to catch any of our sense of community, but the change from their regular routines sometimes gave them enough equanimity to return to their normal lives and better cope. Early on we had one guest whom I particularly liked, and the poem "Manic Gramma" suggests why.

Indeed, I had decided that this woman would be enjoyable in our community, so I was sorry to see her go. I had no firm basis for this expectation except my own pleasure in the connection I made with her in the time she was with us. Her clear enjoyment of the brief time she was in the house made me want to know more of her.

My own sense of community with our residents was strongest when I was on picnics with them. On a day when the weather was good I would sometimes announce, "Picnic for lunch. Everyone who wants to go should make a sack lunch." Most people enjoyed slapping the mayonnaise on their baloney and burrowing in the fridge to find lettuce. Stephanie usually delighted in making an extra sandwich so she would have one to be generous with for some man who didn't make his own. The arrangement was always that I would have drinks to offer when we sat down. On the first picnics I took a can of each of a variety of drinks. It turned out, however, that individual containers were too much for some of my fellow picnickers and not enough for others. I discovered that to be able to pour out the drinks into paper cups as people wanted them gave me a leg up in managing the entire affair. If I poured out drinks only after we were all sitting at a picnic table, it was easier to get everyone to sit for a picnic.

We developed a group of parks that made good picnic spots. One of our favorite places was a path and clearing near the University of Washington arboretum, where my husband and I had walked to talk years ago when we were first dating. The poem "Outing to Foster Island" suggests why it was a favorite spot.

Sometimes a moment would happen on an outing that made a connection for me with one of our residents. Stephanie was one of our most difficult clients when she first came to the house. At first she seemed constantly angry and yelled at the staff and others who she felt were watching her or obstructing her. I volunteered to try to case-manage her, and the first time I had to get a signature from her she stormed about and yelled at me in an attempt to get me to leave her alone. That incident left me leaning against the office door feeling physically weak and wholly lily-livered. The program director suggested that if I didn't enjoy case-managing I needn't persist, and gratefully I turned Stephanie over to someone more professional than I. I continued, however, to attempt to develop a better relationship with her. On an outing to an anthropological museum we finally connected. The poem "Change Happens, But How?" describes that moment.

Stephanie became one of the new residents who cared enough about her fellow housemates to naturally build community within the house. She loved to cook extra quantities and play Lady Bountiful to the others, particularly the men.

Some days it was almost as if the sun or the moon or some vibration from nature got into the whole group on an outing. The good mood that invaded everyone was usually set off by some one person's sense of fun. I could sense it in the van as we drove to the spot we'd chosen. Someone would be high and expansive. To catch the upbeat was always a boost to me as well. The poem "Alki" describes one of those outings.

Money—having money, drawing money each Tuesday—almost always put each person and often the whole group in a good mood. Money empowered, and its power was infectious. No matter how little money anyone had, if they had enough money to walk into a store and choose something, buy it, and carry it out, their spirits soared. Several people particularly enjoyed buying enough of something to share with the whole group. When someone treated the others, the good mood that was engendered built a sense of community. Stephanie was one of those who loved to get money so that she could buy some item and give it away—anything from cigarettes to Cokes to cups of coffee. The poem "After Money Draw" suggests that good mood.

Events like this suggested to me that, indeed, as my husband had told me early in my tenure at the house, the milieu that we on the staff could set the stage for, but not necessarily create ourselves, was all-important. We hoped to give good moments—a sense that our residents not only could cope but wanted to cope—to each mentally ill person who lived at the house, and to those who had graduated to apartments in the surrounding area. We wanted them to enjoy life despite their mental problems, at least sometimes. To that feeling, a sense of community was key.

As for the glove on my heart, it came to be an ever better fit, being an imaginary and protective clinging affair. It protected me from taking my concerns about the mentally ill home with me, and letting them cut too deep. But no protective glove could blunt the affection I came to feel for each of my friends connected to the house.

Alki

Seven of us swish our way to the shoreline
this blue-bright afternoon. Swimming has made
five of us lighter. Money draw has made
six of us spendthrift. The corner store sells
sodas and cigarettes. We sit at a picnic
table on what Carol calls "bird-shit seats."
Her woodpecker cackle peals through our breeze-blown
heads. Tough to light cigarettes in this wind.
Carol and Willie huddle under the neck of his shirt
to light a match. Willie risks a burn for a light.

Suddenly, sitting round that table,
we're like a seven-chambered heart.
We care for each other as usually we don't.
David jokes it's bullshit to say we sit on bird shit.
We discuss the two sorts of fecal material.
Doug, the diviner, declares one's much bigger.
Stephanie claims he doesn't know diddley-poo.
Everyone but Myrtle cackles and chatters.
She sits stark, no Coke or smokes, since she drew
no money. I ask if someone can spare
her a cigarette. David, whose money'd been
cut short—he'd been drinking—offers her one.
Doug won't let him give it, says he has too few,
and hands her one. The under-the-shirt light
doesn't work. Carol lights Myrtle's cigarette
with hers. Rising to walk, we straggle out
single file on the sidewalk. This time more
than usual, our motley crew's a family.

Manic Gramma

Your eyebrows perched on your   craggy face
rise.   You shake   your white, rumpled
head.   Your tone's high, shrill.
"I've been in plenty places for the mentally ill.
At this house,   this one,   I can take
anything   I want from the fridge!
Even cook;   whatever I want.
I can't beliee.e.e.e.e.eve   it."

You ask for a knife.   I check it out
to you,   keep a close watch.
You cut up a whole honeydew,   eat it
kid-like,   plastered across   your mouth,
seeds and all.   The rind falls   to the table.
You haven't bothered   with a plate.
Gnawed through with teeth marks,
the splayed-out rind speaks your delight.

An uproar   invades the house   when I arrive
next morning.   Not five minutes   ago you   hauled off,
melon in one hand   slugged   the program director.
His first time by a gramma.   Your punishment?
A time out.   Go to your room!

Later, wearing magenta satin pajamas   you come out
into the hot,   worried   dining room air.
You return   to your room,   docile,   when we ask you to.
You file a counter request: four soft-boiled eggs.
We boil your breakfast   take your eggs to you.

Later, still wearing   your shocking pink, you appear
calmly...and query me.
"Do you remember the first radio?"
"No," I say, "But as a small child
I heard Amos and Andy."   You squint in awe.
"I remember those first sounds with my family
gathered round that wooden box. The voices
were small miracles.   They were!"
As you speak,   I feel that miracle.

You're drinking herb tea   from a huge Tupperware bowl
when two women come   issue you a summons to court.
This morning, you were violent. The world's afraid of you.
Your daughter's tired   of coping with you.
This house   is too free for you.
My throat catches when I hear   where they will take you.
The system's putting you away.

My job is to listen. I don't have to cross you.
I can be zany with you.
I knew you in a lucid moment. You didn't hit me.
I think you wouldn't hit me. I am free to regret
your going.

Outing to Foster Island

Events when they repeat themselves can
evoke an effect of their former selves.
Forty-seven years ago in May,
I took this same path to Foster Island
on a first date with the man I later married.

Four children and five home countries later
I walk here with eight quirky others whose illnesses
give them odd ideas, wavering resolve.
They ask and I tell them the story of
my first venture in the moon shadows when
I sensed this new gentle man carried whole
bowls of acceptance for me and any word I spoke.

How could I know I'd return to this path
and Myrtle's pop-eyes would fix on a mother
duck with five babies, and her delight would
chant: "When they're little tykes, they bite."

Goose droppings litter the water's edge. Still,
to watch the geese redeems their mess. Sammie
with her usual lassitude allows one
creature to poke its black neck into her
popcorn bag, and its beak pries loose a kernel-
puff avalanche. Another goose snaps at the scatter
on the grass while Samantha coos it on.
Geese give shadow-black bearded David the
jitters. He claims it's a sin to feed them.

Rudy, looking like a beached whale splayed on
the grass, ignores the culprits to plead three
times for more Coke. Kevin bends his huge frame
to pick up plastic connectors. "Small ducks
mustn't strangle." Stately Simon silently observes
the boats go by. I throw the geese
an apple core. If a drake devours it,
will I see the lump move down his neck?

How could I know the acceptance granted
me first on Foster Island would compel
such huge caring for this motley family?

Change Happens, But How?

Something has transformed you.
You used to clobber me with angry
outbursts every time I spoke to you.
Now you yell at new housemates when they
so much as look at you, crowd you, but
you never raise your voice at me. I'm no
longer your case manager. I need nothing
from you now. I used to have to pad
after you with papers for your
signature. Now when you need me to
help find the salt, or take you on an
outing, we connect. Last Friday at
the Burke Museum our four awe-filled eyes
shared the word "Look!" absorbed the
magic fire-red color of that Asian rug.

After Money Draw

After money draw Stephanie asks
for an outing to Alki. She has
the seedy store in mind.
A van full of housemates troop
in its creaky door fixed to buy treats.
Myrtle picks cosmetics,
Samantha chooses chocolates
and typing paper.

Out again, ambling to the lighthouse,
Samantha dubs the chocolates yukkie
and I'm allowed to pass them since they're stale.
Stephanie catches the sharing spirit,
invites us all for coffee at the Luna.
Then she worries her money
won't come up to her bounty and,
planner that she is, proposes to Don
that if her funds fail, he supply the coin
that's missing. Sighing, he agrees.
Five mates go. Only Samantha and Myrtle,
who don't like coffee, decline.

The morning after, the gossip goes
they joshed, they joked at that Luna
table. All round they had a rousing
coffee high.

AFTERWORD

One Parent's Story

by JOANNA MAKI, *Vancouver, Washington*

WE ARE THE FAMILY of "Kevin," one of the more fortunate mentally ill people in our society. He is being helped by a program that is all too rare, the organization about whose residents this book is written.

Our lives were profoundly affected on the morning of December 14, 1993, a date that will forever be in my mind—one week before our very bright, personable son's seventeenth birthday. He went off to school as usual. Within the hour I received a call that he had been picked up by security and was very disoriented. When I arrived at school I was stunned—he was saying wild things and very animated. I later learned he was in the throes of a severe psychotic break.

That day I brought Kevin to a juvenile psychiatric ward—my first experience with the world of mental illness. He was placed under observation in isolation in a room with nothing but a sleeping platform and a blanket. This was to be the first of many hospitalizations for Kevin over the next several years.

I went home and looked up the word "psychosis" in the dictionary—defined in psychiatric terms as disorganized thinking. Thus began my education about mental illness.

My husband came home from work that evening to learn that his son was in a psychiatric ward. Accompanied by our nineteen-year-old daughter, we visited Kevin at the hospital that evening. When we went to his room he was curled up in the fetal position, withdrawn. When he asked if we could stop at the bookstore on the way home when he was released, we told him "of course." When he added that he wanted to get a copy of the book he had written, our daughter burst into tears and left the room. This was her first introduction to the delusional world Kevin had entered.

To that point, we were the most "normal" American family imaginable. We had our two children after ten years of marriage and had thoroughly enjoyed raising them. Our daughter was two years older than Kevin and a sociable, easygoing child. Kevin was full of vim and vigor, a lively, challenging, fun kid. Both got straight A's through grade school. We spent a lot of time with our children, taking trips, hiking, just enjoying being together. I loved every stage throughout their development.

I recall thinking a week or so before Kevin's break that this was a stage I did not enjoy, and I would be glad when it passed. He was irritable, and reacted in unexpected ways. But he was a teenager, and his actions were quite normal for his age. Little did we know that irritability in teenagers is often a sign of depression.

In the few years prior to Kevin's break, my mother had been diagnosed with Alzheimer's, and then I with breast cancer, requiring the usual surgeries and chemotherapy treatments. These events were devastating in themselves, but *this*—our son developing a severe mental illness—this was a nightmare. I think few parents would dream of this occurring. It certainly had never crossed our minds. At the time I likened the experience to a very good book with a shocking, unexpected ending.

As Kevin's illness evolved, the realization slowly came that this was not a passing psychosis. This was a severe illness, and it was not going to go away—ever. His personality was totally gone—all that vim and vigor, humor, energy, even his way of moving and his slim build were gone. The antipsychotic drugs caused a hundred-pound weight gain the first year, so not only did he not act like himself, he looked vastly different from before.

Things were very bumpy during the two years Kevin lived with us. We focused on keeping him occupied and busy, catering to him, thinking he would stabilize and be fine. We found our community mental health system to be vastly inadequate as he quickly ran the gamut of all the support our sizeable community had to offer. And as much as we loved him, our family could not make him well.

When Kevin lived on his own for several months and it quickly became obvious that he was not taking his medications, I feared for him, afraid of what might happen if his actions were interpreted as threatening. I visited the police station near his home to let them know he was mentally ill. When he was finally committed to the state hospital, I was relieved; he was finally safe and receiving needed treatment in the only setting available to him.

While new medications have helped Kevin's old personality shine through again, he is still very tired and desperately wants to be able to do what all twenty-two-year-old men do—drive, have a girlfriend, hold a good job, go to school. Yet he is ambivalent about his wants. He no longer has confidence in his abilities because of the effects of both the medications and the illness. Even though his symptoms have lessened, stressful situations still cause a certain degree of mental disorganization.

The six years since our son became ill have been both a heartbreaking and hopeful time. Our main concerns are that he be safe and that he have a life that is secure and satisfying. His future is very tenuous and dependent on community support and on his taking his medication. As time passes I can see Kevin's frustration with the need to lower his expectations despite his greater-than-average intelligence. He wants his life to be as it once was—yet he is an unusually compassionate and sensitive person. While on one hand I feel bad that he is strapped with this most serious mental illness, on the other hand I wonder whether he would have these wonderful caring qualities if his mind were "normal." It is as though he can see right through the exterior trappings to the inner needs of people around him. We are so proud of the person he is!

I have learned a lot about mental illness—that mentally ill people are our beloved family members, that when they act out it is often because they are fearful, that they are tortured by thoughts over which they have no control, that they are terribly lonely, and that the medications are awful to take but absolutely necessary. Rather than being shunned by the rest of us, they deserve our respect and compassion.

I hope the reader of this book comes away with an understanding that these are people who have tremendous roadblocks in life—they are worthwhile beings with the desire to contribute to society—they are more like us than they are different.